Studies in Musical Genesis and Structure

General Editor: Lewis Lockwood, Harvard University

Studies in Musical Genesis and Structure
General Editor: Lewis Lockwood, Harvard University

Beethoven's 'Appassionata' Sonata

MARTHA FROHLICH

CLARENDON PRESS · OXFORD
1991

Oxford University Press, Walton Street, Oxford OX2 6DP
Oxford New York Toronto
Delhi Bombay Calcutta Madras Karachi
Petaling Jaya Singapore Hong Kong Tokyo
Nairobi Dar es Salaam Cape Town
Melbourne Auckland
and associated companies in
Berlin Ibadan

Oxford is a trade mark of Oxford University Press

Published in the United States
by Oxford University Press, New York

British Library Cataloguing in Publication Data
Data available

Library of Congress Cataloging in Publication Data
Data available

ISBN 0–19–816189–1

Set by Hope Services (Abingdon), Ltd.
Printed in Great Britain by
Biddles Ltd., Guildford and King's Lynn

To Bathia Churgin and Newton Frohlich

Editor's Preface

Historical musicology has recently witnessed vigorous efforts to deepen understanding of the means by which composers of various periods and traditions brought their works to realization. In part this trend has resulted from renewed and intensive study of the manuscript sources of works by many of the major figures in Western music history, especially those for whom new and authoritative complete editions are being undertaken. In part it has arisen from the desire to establish more cogent and precise claims about the formative background of individual works than could be accomplished by more general stylistic study. In many cases, the fortunate survival of much of the composer's working materials—sketches, drafts, composing scores, corrected copies, and the like—has stimulated this approach on a scale that no one could have imagined a century ago, when Gustav Nottebohm's pioneering studies of Beethoven's sketches and drafts first appeared.

This series provides a number of short monographs, each dealing with a single work by an important composer. The main focus will be on the genesis of the work from its known antecedent stages, so far as these can be determined from the sources. In each case the genesis of the work will be connected to an analytical overview of the final version. Every monograph will be written by a specialist, and, apart from the general theme of the series, no artificial uniformity will be imposed. The individual character of both work and evidence, as well as the author's special viewpoint, will dictate differences in emphasis and treatment. Thus some of these studies may stress the combination of sketch evidence and analysis, while others may shift the emphasis to the position of the work within its genre and context. Although no such series could possibly aim at being comprehensive, it will deal with a representative body of important works by composers of stature across the centuries.

Martha Frohlich's new study of Beethoven's 'Appassionata' Sonata, Op. 57, should be welcomed. As one of the two most famous piano sonatas of Beethoven's middle years (the other, of course, is the 'Waldstein'), this work has received its share of commentary and analysis in larger studies of Beethoven's piano sonatas or of his work as a whole, but has never been the subject of a full-length monograph in English. Dr Frohlich's book, based on her study of the surviving sketches and the autograph manuscript, deepens our understanding of the compositional origins of the 'Appassionata'. It demonstrates convincingly that certain elements in this powerful three-movement sonata were firmly fixed at an early stage and that others—including, surprisingly, the lyrical second subject of the first movement—were added later. This latter point, known in a general way to Nottebohm and others but never before well documented, is just one of the detailed but significant compositional changes that this study brings to light. By casting new light on the specific background of this powerful and, as Tovey called it, 'eminently tragic' work, this book illuminates its final form, shape, and stature.

Harvard University   Lewis Lockwood

Acknowledgements

I am indebted to many people for help and advice in this endeavour. My special thanks go to Sieghard Brandenburg, for the generous amount of time he devoted to assisting with certain difficult problems of transcription, and for reading part of the manuscript and offering valuable suggestions; to Alan Tyson, for advice regarding problems related to dating the Op. 57 sketches in Mendelssohn 15; to Jan LaRue, for his thoughtful reading of Part I of the manuscript; and to Lewis Lockwood, for helpful counsel.

I am grateful to Dr Rudolf Elvers of the Staatsbibliothek Preussischer Kulturbesitz Berlin, Musikabteilung, for permission to work with the sketchbook Mendelssohn 15, and to Dr Hans-Günter Klein for the authorization to include copies of the original pages in this study. I am also grateful to the Bibliothèque Nationale, Paris, for allowing me access to the autograph of Op. 57, and for permission to reproduce certain pages from that document.

My deep appreciation goes to Beth Shamgar, for her repeated willingness to offer fresh reactions and cogent editorial advice; to John Rothgeb, for making his excellent translation of Heinrich Schenker's essay on Op. 57 available to me; and to Roger Kamien, for helpful suggestions. I would also like to thank Svetlana Gordon for preparing all the music examples, and Judy Goldberg for typing the manuscript.

Portions of this book have appeared in an earlier form in the *Israel Studies in Musicology* and the *Beethoven Newsletter*; I would like to thank the current editors of those publications for permission to reuse the material.

This book is dedicated to two people: Bathia Churgin, who by her own impeccable scholarship, devoted teaching, and warm friendship has been both a guide and an inspiration; and my husband, Newton Frohlich, whose unfailing encouragement and support has made it possible.

Israel   M.F.
December 1990

Contents

List of Figures

List of Tables

Introduction

One of Beethoven's most celebrated piano sonatas is the monumental Op. 57 in F minor, known as the 'Appassionata'.[1] The genesis of this sonata, which springs from his prolific middle period (*c.* 1802–*c.* 1814), can be traced to 1804–5, when Beethoven's labours on his opera *Leonore* occupied a central position in his creative life. It was a time shaped by a remarkable outpouring of great works, as even a partial list of compositions completed or well advanced in the years 1803–6 shows: the 'Eroica' Symphony, Op. 55 (1803–4), the 'Waldstein' Sonata, Op. 53 (1803–4); the oratorio *Christus am Oelberge*, Op. 85 (1803; revised 1804); the Triple Concerto, Op. 56 (1803–4); the 'Appassionata' Sonata, Op. 57 (1804–5); *Fidelio*, Op. 72, titled *Leonore* (1st version with *Leonore* Overture No. 2, 1804–5; 2nd version with *Leonore* Overture No. 3, 1805–6; final version with *Fidelio* Overture in 1814); the Fourth Piano Concerto, Op. 58 (1805–6); the 'Rasumovsky' String Quartets, Op. 59 (1805–6); the Violin Concerto, Op. 61 (1806); the Fourth Symphony, Op. 60 (1806); and, finally, the Fifth Symphony, Op. 67 (1804 preliminary sketches; mainly in 1807–8).[2]

Actual work on Op. 57 may have begun in the summer of 1804, although the first edition of the sonata appeared only much later, in February 1807.[3] Beethoven's vigorous compositional activity during this period found a parallel in his increasing involvement with the young widow, Countess Josephine Deym (1779–1821). Their relationship reached its most intense phase in late 1804 and early 1805, when it is thought that Beethoven was working concentratedly on the 'Appassionata'.[4] By 1807, however, their feelings had cooled and

---

[1] As noted in Georg Kinsky, *Das Werk Beethovens: Thematisch-bibliographisches Verzeichnis seiner sämtlichen vollendeten Kompositionen*, completed and ed. Hans Halm (Munich and Duisburg, 1955), 135, the title 'Appassionata' did not originate with Beethoven, but with the Hamburg publisher Cranz, in a four-hand arrangement of the sonata he published in June 1838.

[2] The dates given here are taken from the worklist compiled by Douglas Johnson in Joseph Kerman and Alan Tyson, *The New Grove Beethoven* (New York, 1983; rev. edn. of 'Beethoven', in *The New Grove Dictionary of Music and Musicians*, ed. Stanley Sadie, London, 1980), 158–89.

[3] For details of publication, title, reprints, etc., see Kinsky–Halm, pp. 135–6.

[4] Traces of their relationship appear in thirteen letters written by Beethoven to Josephine, first published in Joseph Schmidt-Görg, *Dreizehn unbekannte Briefe an*

in 1810 Josephine remarried. Nevertheless, Beethoven maintained his long-standing friendship with her family and dedicated the 'Appassionata' to her brother, Count Franz von Brunsvik (1777–1849).[5]

From the beginning the 'Appassionata' was greeted with enthusiasm. The new technical challenges as well as the special beauties of the sonata were recognized by the reviewer in the *Allgemeine musikalische Zeitung*. Commenting on the first movement, he wrote that in this case it is 'worth the trouble to struggle with the severe difficulties, as well as with the far-fetched strangeness of Beethoven's style!'[6] Czerny reports that Beethoven considered Op. 57 to be his 'greatest sonata up to the period when he had composed his Op. 106'.[7] Czerny's own praise of the sonata, as 'the most complete development of a powerful and colossal idea',[8] might well serve as a standard for the consistently favourable reception accorded to this work in the nineteenth and twentieth centuries.[9]

Given the sustained appeal the 'Appassionata' has held for analysts and performers alike, we are fortunate that the autograph as well as fourteen pages of sketches for the sonata survive. While there are many gaps in the sketches, the extant material, particularly for the first movement, is sufficiently comprehensive to permit us to glimpse the evolution of a good part of the material of the sonata. Furthermore, the autograph adds an extra dimension to our efforts; changes occurring

Josephine Gräfin Deym (Bonn, 1957). The letters are translated in Emily Anderson (ed. and trans.), *The Letters of Beethoven* (New York, 1961), i, Letters Nos. 97, 102, 103, 110, 112, 113, 114, 115, 125, 142, 151, 154, and 156 (hereafter abbreviated as, for example, Anderson No. 97).

[5] Count Franz von Brunsvik also received the dedication of Beethoven's Fantasy for Piano, Op. 77 (1809). Josephine's sister, Therese, received the dedication of the Piano Sonata, Op. 78 (1809). The piano duet, Six Variations on 'Ich denke dein', WoO74 (1799; 1803), is dedicated to both Josephine and Therese, who were Beethoven's piano pupils in the years 1799–1804.

[6] See the *Allgemeine musikalische Zeitung*, 9 (1 Apr. 1807), col. 433: 'aber wahrhaftig, ist hier auch der Mühe werth, mit den argen Schwierigkeiten nicht nur, sondern auch mit mancher Anwandlung des Unwillens über gesuchte Wunderlichkeiten und Bizarrerien, zu kämpfen!'

[7] Carl Czerny, *On the Proper Performance of All Beethoven's Works for the Piano*; chs 2 and 3 of *The Complete Theoretical and Practical Piano Forte School*, Op. 500, iv; facsimile of the English edn. (London, 1842), ed. Paul Badura-Skoda (Vienna, 1970), 58.

[8] Ibid. 58.

[9] Early recognition of the popular appeal of the 'Appassionata' is reflected in Clara Wieck's inclusion of this work in her Vienna début. In response to her performance of the sonata, Austria's leading poet, Franz Grillparzer, wrote a poem of praise published on 9 January 1838 in the *Wiener Zeitschrift für Kunst*. See Nancy B. Reich, *Clara Schumann, the Artist and the Woman* (Ithaca and London, 1985), 25.

in this document, especially in the finale, show how Beethoven's determination to deepen and refine his music stretched even into the last compositional phase.

The present study focuses on an investigation of these manuscript sources. Implicit in this undertaking is the belief that Beethoven's sketches are intrinsically valuable, as positive creative acts, worthy of our attention even when we cannot relate them to a completed work. Yet, while the sketches give us a broad view of Beethoven's compositional fluency and abundant musical imagination, it is difficult to evaluate them in a vacuum. In order to put the multiple possibilities explored in the sketches into perspective, we need some standard of measure. The only reliable standard that affords us an opportunity to grasp why Beethoven preferred one option over another is the final version. By attempting to understand his intentions there, we can get a sense of the underlying basis for his compositional choices. For this reason, I have prefaced my discussion of the sketches with a review of salient points in the finished work.

The sketch discussion is organized by movement, and within each movement by section. Because of the sporadic and sometimes fragmentary nature of many of the sketches, determining chronology is frequently puzzling; but where it seems possible to order the sketches, as for example in the coda sketches for the first movement, I have attempted to do so. Other questions pursued here include the following:

1. From the sketches we have, what sections of the composition appear to have received special attention?
2. Are any parts of the final version conspicuously absent or different in the sketches?
3. Is there any material of significance in the sketches that never appears in the final version?
4. How do revisions in the autograph fit into the compositional process?

In the course of this study it will become apparent that, while many definitive characteristics seem to have been fixed from the start, other important ideas emerged only gradually. The primary theme of the first movement with its transposition to the Neapolitan, for example, appears in the earliest sketches and its content changes little throughout. On the other hand, the second theme in A flat major, whose presence as a lyrical counterbalance to the stormy opening seems indispensable to the expression and structure of the whole, is completely absent from the first exposition draft, seeming to arise full-blown only at a later stage.

While dramatic changes such as the sudden interpolation of this theme are striking, it is in the continuous flow of small adjustments that we sense most keenly the full weight of Beethoven's shaping hand. That he was aware of how even modest alterations in melodic contour, harmonic rhythm, phrase organization, or dynamics could affect the integrity of the whole is reflected in a statement he once made to the publisher, George Thomson. Beethoven wrote, 'I am profoundly convinced that every change of detail changes the character of the composition'.[10]

[10] Anderson No. 405, dated 19 Feb. 1813: 'Je ne suis pas accoutumé de retoucher mes compositions; Je ne l'ai jamais fait, pénétré de la vérité que tout changement partiel altère le caractère de la composition.'

PART I. THE FINAL VERSION

1. Overview and First Movement

OVERVIEW

Of the many observations that have been made about Beethoven's 'Appassionata' Sonata, two in particular seem to describe its special qualities. First, there is the sense of unity and integration that permeates the work. This coherence is unusual, because it operates in nearly every musical element and on every structural level, both in the detail of individual movements and across the whole. Furthermore, motion, from the darkness of the first movement, into the light and peace of the second, and, then, through a vivid tempo connection, into the *perpetuum mobile* of the finale, creates a remarkably satisfying psychological progression, that is supported by Beethoven's handling of both tonal and motivic relationships.

Secondly, there is the underlying tension generated in the first movement between structure and content: the passionate intensity of the themes seems barely contained by the taut, almost rigid symmetry of the architectural frame. Special pianistic effects contribute to the sense of unprecedented power: the emphasis on extreme textural contrasts and bass sonorities for creating mood; the sudden cascades of sound covering the total range of the piano; and the percussive ostinato binding the development and recapitulation.

Yet these and other characteristic aspects of the 'Appassionata' are either anticipated or echoed in some of Beethoven's other works from the early and middle periods. The choice of F minor as tonic, for example, links Op. 57 with two forerunners: the Piano Sonata, WoO 47 No. 2 (pub. 1783) and Op. 2 No. 1 (1793–5). The first movement of the early Bonn sonata is most often cited in connection with the first movement of the Sonata Pathétique, Op. 13 (1797–8); both open with a slow introduction which returns in the development, while in both the primary theme ascends through two octaves in the right hand over a tonic pedal in the bass. As in Op. 57, however, the F minor key evokes the emphatic use of the Neapolitan harmony (in m. 6 of the slow introduction). The opening of the first movement of Op. 2 No. 1, with its triadic primary theme and forceful dynamic contrasts, calls to mind the beginning of Op. 57; furthermore, in both cases the secondary theme retains a rhythmic and melodic similarity with the primary one, unfolding from an initial inversion of the same triadic shape.

Two slightly later works, again in the same key, share the pre-occupation in the 'Appassionata' with Neapolitan relationships: the *Egmont* Overture, Op. 84 (1809–10) and the Quartet, Op. 95 (1810). In the first movements of both Op. 95 and Op. 57 the move to the Neapolitan in unison texture forms the initial gesture, and has long-range implications for structure; there is also a similar emphasis on D flat major as an important key in the first movement. In Op. 84 the sound of the Neapolitan appears as a local effect, reserved for the second theme (in A flat major, mm. 92–7; when the theme returns in D flat major in the recapitulation, its Neapolitan colour remains intact, mm. 235–40).

Prominent Neapolitan formations in other minor-key works also suggest Op. 57. In the finale of the Piano Sonata in C sharp minor, Op. 27 No. 2 (1801), the second theme moves suddenly to a virtuosic passage beginning on the Neapolitan sixth of the dominant minor (m. 33). The theme recurs with Neapolitan colour three times: in the development (F sharp minor to G major, mm. 75–80); in the recapitulation; and in the coda, where closure is signalled by the appearance of the Neapolitan as part of a cadential progression in the tonic (mm. 177–90).[1] In the first movement of the Violin Sonata in C minor, Op. 30 No. 2 (1801–2), a Neapolitan progression highlights the final appearance of the second theme in the coda (mm. 222–5). Additional procedures in this movement also anticipate events in the first movement of Op. 57. Once again there is a primary theme opening in a unison texture; interconnected primary and secondary themes, where the triadic shape of one is an inversion of the other; use of non-repeating sonata form; and focus on internal third relationships in the tonal plan of the development, which in each case begins with a series of descending major thirds.[2] Finally, the opening of the Quartet in E minor, Op. 59 No. 2 (1806), begins, like Opp. 57 and 95, with an immediate restatement of the opening phrase in the Neapolitan.

Beethoven's exploitation of an initial chromatic inflection for creating long-range continuity found in Op. 57 has a precedent in the first movement of the Piano Sonata in D major, Op. 10 No. 3 (1798),

---

[1] On the generative power of the Neapolitan chord, see Harold Thompson, 'An Evolutionary View of Neapolitan Formations in Beethoven's Pianoforte Sonatas', *College Music Symposium*, 20 (1980), 144–62.

[2] From Op. 29 onwards Beethoven increasingly explored third relationships as an alternative to fifth relationships. A complete spiral of descending major thirds occurs also in Op. 24/II/mm. 37–44.

where the half-step motion A♮–A♯ in m. 20 carries harmonic implications in every part of the form. In the exposition, A♯ functions as a leading tone to B minor for the transition (m. 23); in the development, A♯ becomes B♭ for a sustained passage in this key (m. 133); in the recapitulation, A♯ functions as the raised fourth degree in E minor (m. 202); and, in the coda, the play on this note is emphasized by *sf* indications under a repeated B♭, resolved first as an augmented sixth to V (m. 320), and, finally, as A♯, the leading tone to vi in D major.[3]

Another distinctive feature of Op. 57 is the way in which the keys of each movement combine to form a larger harmonic progression: F minor in the first movement moves to D flat major in the second; the second movement closes with a diminished-seventh chord that elides into the off-tonic beginning of the finale, where this chord moves to a dominant seventh before falling to the tonic. The progression outlined is thus i–VI–V$^0_9$–V$_7$–i in F minor. Similar broad cadential formulations mark the key plans of other works in this period. Two examples from the piano literature are the 'Waldstein' Sonata, Op. 53 (in C major: I; IV–V; I) and the Fourth Piano Concerto, Op. 58 (in G major: I; vi; IV–I).

The linking of the second and third movements of Op. 57 reflects Beethoven's growing interest in intensifying continuity within a cycle during this period. Beginning with the 'attacca' indications joining inner movements in the Piano Sonatas, Op. 27 Nos. 1 and 2, he explored multiple ways of creating connections. Among the many different solutions he achieved, a few in particular seem analogous to the situation in Op. 57, in which the slow movement ends with an incomplete cadence, moving into a transitional passage prefacing the actual start of the next movement.[4] In the third movement of the Quartet, Op. 59 No. 1, the trill on the dominant in the violin overlaps with the beginning of the finale, which displays an initial harmonic ambiguity that only resolves after eighteen measures. In the second movement of the Quartet, Op. 95, Beethoven touches on the tonic, but then closes on a diminished-seventh chord with a fermata; an 'attacca' indication leads to the next movement, which begins off the

[3] As pointed out in Douglas Johnson, '1794–1795: Decisive Years in Beethoven's Early Development', in *Beethoven Studies*, iii, ed. Alan Tyson (Cambridge, 1982), 27.

[4] The two quartet examples come from the cogent review of various types of inter-movement connections by Lewis Lockwood, 'Beethoven and the Problem of Closure: Some Examples from the Middle-Period Chamber Music', in Sieghard Brandenburg and Helmut Loos (eds.), *Beethoven-Symposion, Bonn 1984* (Munich, 1987), 254–72. Other middle-period works with connections between movements include: Opp. 53, 61, 67, 68, 69, 73, 74, 81a, 96, and 97.

tonic, delaying tonal stability until m. 17. A written-out tempo connection, analogous to the gradual acceleration delineated in mm. 1–20 of the finale of Op. 57, closes the slow movement of the Triple Concerto, Op. 56.

As a precedent for the extreme registral contrasts, rich texture, and sonorous pianistic effects in the first movement of Op. 57, we can look to the first movement of the Sonata Pathétique. Here we find a similar predilection for the use of a tremolo accompaniment to lend tension to the primary theme, and the purposeful exploitation of ambiguity in the diminished-seventh chord to shape the form (see the end of the slow introduction, m. 10; the beginning of the development, m. 135; the close of the retransition, mm. 187–93; and the start of the coda, mm. 293–4).

Finally, Op. 57 shares certain structural parallels with its immediate precedessor, the Piano Sonata in F major, Op. 54, sketched at the beginning of Mendelssohn 15. These include:

1. repeating the development and recapitulation as a means of extending the internal proportions (in the second movement of Op. 54 and the finale of Op. 57);
2. intensifying the return of the primary theme at the opening of the recapitulation by placing it over a rhythmically active pedal-point in the bass (in the second movement of Op. 54 the theme enters over a broken tonic pedal; in the first movement of Op. 57 the dominant pedal overlaps from the end of the development, acting as an ostinato);
3. integrating the sonata by means of inter-movement connections (in Op. 54 this is accomplished by recalling transition material from the first movement in a transition area of the second movement; in Op. 57 all three movements share common motives; the second and third movements are harmonically interlocked, and the first and third movements share structural affinities);
4. accelerating the tempo in the coda in order to place more weight on the end of the movement (the second movement of Op. 54 and the outer movements of Op. 57 all include tempo accelerations).

As a prelude to discussing the sketches and autograph, let us now turn to an analysis of the final version. The following remarks, which draw on previous studies of the sonata made by Heinrich Schenker,[5]

[5] Heinrich Schenker, 'Beethoven: Sonata Opus 57', *Tonwille*, 7 (1924), 3–33. I am grateful to John Rothgeb for making his excellent translation of this essay available to me.

Rudolf Réti,[6] Jürgen Uhde,[7] and others, are not intended to present a new picture of the work, but rather to summarize its essential features. For the analysis, I have adopted the approach of Jan LaRue.[8] The LaRue framework is particularly useful for dealing with the sketches, because it provides specific terminology, not only for larger functions, but also for smaller aspects such as phrase, subphrase, and motive.

The following symbols proposed by LaRue have been used to indicate thematic functions: O (introductory material); P (themes in the primary key area); T (transitional themes connecting the two main key areas); S (themes presented in the secondary key area); and K (cadential or closing themes). If there is more than one theme, they are labelled consecutively, as, for example, $1P$, $2P$, etc. In addition, the symbol PT refers to a thematic area that leads from P to T; KT refers to a transition from the end of K to the beginning of the development; finally, N identifies new material occurring after the exposition. Other LaRue symbols used here include the indications a, b, and c for phrases, x, y, and z for subphrases, and m for motive. Superscripts are used to indicate the return of an element in varied form. Thus, for example, the presentation of the first primary theme in the finale of Op. 57 is designated $1P$, while its varied repetition in mm. 28–35 is designated as $1P^1$.

Two additional terms incorporated from LaRue are: 'module', which signifies 'the pervading or characteristic growth segment' (*Guidelines*, Cue Sheet for Style Analysis); and 'surface rhythm', which covers 'all relationships of durations, assumed to be approximately as represented by the symbols of notation' (*Guidelines*, p. 91).

In the analytical tables, and in the text when several keys are listed in succession, major keys are indicated by capital letters and minor keys by lower-case letters; similarly, major chords are indicated by upper-case roman numerals and minor chords by lower-case roman numerals. An indication such as V/V identifies a secondary dominant; an augmented-sixth chord is abbreviated as A_6. Upper-case roman numerals appearing after opus numbers, and/or before measure numbers, indicate the specific number referred to, as in Op. 57/III/ mm. 1–2. Definite pitches use the system on the next page:

[6] Rudolf Réti, *Thematic Patterns in the Sonatas of Beethoven*, ed. Deryck Cooke (New York, 1967), 97–126.

[7] Jürgen Uhde, *Beethovens Klaviermusik*, iii (Stuttgart, 1974), 188–225.

[8] LaRue's approach is outlined in his book, *Guidelines for Style Analysis* (New York, 1970).

FF   C   B   c   b   c¹   b¹   c²   b²   c³   c⁴

FIRST MOVEMENT

The first movement of Op. 57 exhibits Beethoven's mastery of architecture on a grand scale. He has carefully balanced its overall shape in a number of different ways. First, the proportions of each main section—exposition, development, recapitulation, and coda—are remarkably similar in length.[9] In addition, each of these sections is clearly articulated melodically and dynamically by opening with a statement of the primary theme in a low register. Moreover, Beethoven closes the movement with an augmented version of the head motive from the primary theme in the same register in which it began. The low F in the bass at m. 262 matches that found in m., while the c^2 in the right hand corresponds to the soprano note in m. 3.[10]

A number of distinctive sonorities enhance our perception of the structure and, simultaneously, create a mood of brooding intensity. The low, hollow sound of the unison texture opening both exposition and development functions as a kind of matrix from which the primary theme unfolds. The pairing of a motive from this theme, placed in the bass, with a tremolo accompaniment above brings an aura of mysterious excitement to every main division of the form (see mm. 64, 79–80, 203–9, 257–61). Extended arpeggios sweep across the whole range of the piano at crucial points (see, for example, mm. 14–15, 123–9, 218–34), and dynamic extremes frequently occur in sharp juxtaposition.[11] Finally, the predominance of the minor mode (only 75 of the total 262 measures of the movement are in the major) lends a dark cast to the whole movement.

[9] The division between sections is sometimes ambiguous because Beethoven uses several techniques to create continuity, such as linking measures, or elision. I have divided the sections as follows: Exposition, mm. 1–65; link, m. 66; development, mm. 67–134; link, m. 135; recapitulation, mm. 136–204; coda (elision), mm. 204–62. Another famous middle-period work with similarly symmetrical proportions is the first movement of the Fifth Symphony (1807–8). There, the exposition and development are both 124 mm. long; the recapitulation is 125 mm., and the coda is 128 mm.

[10] Schenker, 'Beethoven: Sonata Opus 57', p. 13, notes that Beethoven begins and ends the movement with the fifth of the tonic chord.

[11] See, for example, *pp–ff*, mm. 16–17; *ff–p*, mm. 20–1; *f–sf–p*, mm. 42–3. Also striking is the unusual *ppp* in the final measure. This dynamic, rare in Beethoven, is found also at the close of the *Minore* in Op. 7/III.

Beethoven's long-range planning of climax regions further shapes the movement. The most extended peak occurs towards the end of the coda, where seventeen measures of virtuosic figuration culminate in a tempo acceleration (mm. 218–38). The section that follows presents the tonal resolution of unstable motives from the primary and secondary themes, and also introduces a new, rhythmically propulsive closing theme (mm. 249–56).

This terminal climax is prefigured by three smaller ones, each of which articulates the conclusion of a main section. The first occurs in mm. 51–60, where we find the fastest surface and harmonic rhythm of the exposition, the melodic apex (cb⁴ in m. 60), and the most sustained period of dynamic stress (*f* or *ff*). The second begins with the textural change at the start of the retransition (m. 123). Here, the bass, which has previously climbed two octaves, becomes part of a sustained diminished-seventh chord, while the tessitura continues to rise at a fortissimo level. The third climax, at the close of the recapitulation, has its analogue in the exposition; however, harmonic, rhythmic, and dynamic intensifications from earlier parts of the recapitulation render this recall more powerful than its original statement (these intensifications are outlined below on p. 24).

Beethoven sets these events on broad tonal pillars: F minor, the tonic key; A flat major/minor, the secondary key;[12] and D flat major, which serves both as the 'point of furthest remove' in the development,[13] and the key signalling thematic and tonal resolution in the coda. Within this basic scheme the Neapolitan relationship, F–Gb, exerts a critical influence on modulatory patterns.[14] Beethoven establishes its importance in the opening of the sonata, where the second phrase of the primary theme is a half-step transposition of the first. Later, the approach to the secondary key is achieved by an abrupt, half-step shift in the outer voices (m. 23). Similarly, the turn to E (or F flat) major at the beginning of the development involves half-step motion from D♯ to E (mm. 66–7); the series of modulations in mm. 79–92 show half-step motion in the bass, from the tonic of the old key to the

---

[12] The use of a tonal plan with modal contrast in the *S–K* area has a precedent in Clementi's Piano Sonata in G minor, Op. 34 No. 2 (*c.*1795). Two earlier works from Beethoven's middle period featuring an *S* area in major followed by a *K* area in minor are Op. 29/I and Op. 31 No. 1/I.

[13] The term 'point of furthest remove' comes from Leonard Ratner, *Classic Music: Expression, Form, and Style* (New York, 1980), 225. It indicates the harmony in the development that initiates the change of direction 'from a centrifugal motion (away from I) to a centripedal motion (toward I)'.

[14] This aspect of the analysis is indebted to David Epstein, *Beyond Orpheus: Studies in Musical Structure* (Cambridge, Mass., 1979), 213–31. For Epstein's remarks on Op. 57/I, see ibid. 228–31.

seventh of the new key. Subsequent modulations in the development and coda follow a similar pattern.[15]

The Neapolitan relationship also affects the melodic shape of other themes in the exposition.[16] In the secondary theme, for example, the Neapolitan of A flat major (m. 42), emphasized by a sudden dynamic intensification, works together with an augmentation of the consequent phrase of the theme to signal a modal shift back to the minor. Beethoven highlights the same chord in the closing area, this time in root position, with both a more exaggerated deceleration in the surface rhythm of the left hand, and increased dynamic stress (note the *ff* in mm. 53 and 57, and the sudden change from sixteenths to a dotted half-note on B♭♭). He gives this harmonic relationship a subtle twist in the first part of the development (mm. 71–2), where the progression, minor tonic to major Neapolitan in F minor, becomes major tonic to minor supertonic in E major. Finally, in the coda it is a Neapolitan sixth that initiates the main climax of the movement (m. 218).

One other sonority that resonates throughout this movement is the diminished-seventh chord, E♮–G–B♭–D♭. It often emerges at points of extreme tension, to highlight arrival on the dominant, or preface a recall of the semitone motive D♭–C (see, for example, mm. 14–15, 123–31, 149–50, and 238). Similarly, the reinterpretation of this chord marks the entrance into the secondary theme and the confirmation of its key. In m. 32 the pitch D♭ is transformed, so that it no longer functions as the sixth degree in F minor, but becomes instead the fourth degree in the new key of A flat major.[17]

In conjunction with harmony, recurring thematic elements integrate the main sections. Heinrich Schenker and others have shown how motives from the primary theme generate material for much of the entire sonata.[18] Some of the most obvious motivic relationships in the first movement (illustrated in Ex. 1) are listed below.

1.   *Pax* consists of a downward arpeggio from dominant to tonic, followed by an inversion, rising from the third to the tonic (mm. 1–2). This motive becomes a source for the secondary

[15] See mm. 112–13, from D flat major to B flat minor, where the left hand moves from A♭ to A♮; mm. 116–17, from B flat minor to G flat major, where the bass moves from F to G♭; and mm. 205–6, from F minor to D flat major, where the bass moves from F to G♭.

[16] Epstein, *Beyond Orpheus*, p. 228.

[17] On the defining role of the diminished-seventh chord in this movement, see Patricia Carpenter, '*Grundgestalt* as Tonal Function', *Music Theory Spectrum*, 3 (1983), 19.

[18] See Schenker, 'Beethoven: Sonata Opus 57', pp. 3–33; Réti, *Thematic Patterns*, pp. 97–112.

Ex. 1. Main motives, first movement, exposition

theme (*S*, m. 35), which begins with its inversion.[19] As if to call attention to this relationship, Beethoven begins both themes from the identical pitch, c'. *Pax* also gives rise to the melodic tremolo that becomes a characteristic accompaniment pattern. This derivation is most transparent in mm. 78–9, where the up-beat for the left-hand melody and the notes of the right-hand accompaniment share the same pitches, B♮–G, although in different registers.[20]

2. *Pay* consists of a rising and falling whole step, C–D♮–C (as in mm. 4–5) or half-step, C–D♭–C (as in m. 23, with resolution to C delayed until m. 35). This neighbour-tone figure generates the melodic outline of a number of themes: the transition theme (*T*, mm. 24–7, on B♭–C♭–B♭; in diminution as a 'sigh motive' in mm. 27–8); the new development theme (*N*, mm. 105–9);[21] and the new closing theme in the coda (*NK* mm. 251, 254–6). Beethoven also embeds an inversion of this motive in *S* (see the dotted quarters in the right hand, mm. 36–7, on A♭–G–A♭; and similarly mm. 38–9, on C–B♭–C).

3. *Pb* (mm. 9–13) includes both a prolongation of *Pay* material and its compression into the semitone motive, D♭–C (m. 10). This motive (*Pbm*) permeates the musical fabric at all levels, both at original pitch and in transposition. Its tapping rhythm (♫♩) is suggested in the melodic rhythm of the first closing theme (*1K*, mm. 51–60) and, varied and in diminution, in the right-hand accompaniment of the second closing theme (*2K*, mm. 61–3, as ♪ ♪ ♫).[22]

4. The entire first phrase of *P* gives rise to the counter-statement

---

[19] Schenker ('Beethoven: Sonata Opus 57', p. 6) claims that the main melodic motive of *S* is a descending third (C–B♭–A♭, and D♭–C–B♭), thus suggesting this theme anticipates the descending third motion in the melodic line of *1K* (m. 51, the right hand, in the second group of sixteenths). However, since these third progressions in *S* are neither rhythmically emphasized nor rhythmically parallel, I feel the neighbour-tone motive is more outstanding.

[20] D. Blagoy suggests that the different stemming for these notes in the autograph—up for the up-beat to the melody in the left hand, and down for the accompaniment in the right hand—illustrates the transfer from one function to another. See his 'Appassionata', *Sovetskaja muzyka*, 34 (1970), 85. I am grateful to Joachim Braun for translating this article for me.

[21] Schenker 'Beethoven: Sonata Opus 57', p. 11) emphasizes the descending third motion here, rather than the neighbour-tone, because he sees this theme as preparation for the same motion in the upcoming presentation of *S*.

[22] Some other Beethoven works composed between 1804 and 1808 similarly unified by recurrence of a tapping rhythm are: Op. 58/I, Op. 59 No. 1/II, Op. 61/I, and Op. 67/I.

(*PT*, mm. 17–23), where tonic or dominant chords are interpolated between segments of the original opening phrase.[23]

The same thematic material generates momentum as the movement progresses. Two aspects of Beethoven's strategy are crucial in this respect. First, he sustains a sense of drive toward the coda by delaying the harmonic and melodic resolution of the unstable *Pb* motive until m. 239. Second, he sets in motion a gradual and ultimately radical character change in *S*. Because this extended transformation comprises a central narrative thread of the movement, it will be described in some detail.[24]

In order to understand the nature of the alterations in *S*, it is first useful to define it in relation to its precursor, *P*. If we try to isolate the signal characteristics of *S* in its initial appearance, we can see that, despite the presence of shared melodic and harmonic features, Beethoven casts these two themes as opposites (see Table 1).

TABLE 1. *Themes P and S, first movement, exposition, compared*

P (mm. 1–16)	*S* (mm. 35–46)
Minor	Major/minor
Phrase structure is developmental; each phrase seems to grow from the preceding one.	Phrase structure is more balanced: *a + a'*; *Sa* begins and ends with the same pitches, c'–eb'.
Harmony is chromatic and unstable; the tonic is heard only at the beginning; the theme moves directly to the Neapolitan, and emphasis thereafter is on V, yielding an open effect.	Harmony is diatonic and more stable; emphasis on I and V; *Sa* ends on the tonic (m. 39).
Highly punctuated by frequent rests; extreme contrasts in register, texture, dynamics, and rhythm.	Legato; mostly soft dynamics; overall texture of melody/chordal accompaniment is maintained.
Sturm und Drang style.	Lyrical style, marked 'dolce'.

[23] Schenker ('Beethoven: Sonata Opus 57', p. 6) suggests that these insertions prepare us for a larger interpolation: he views the transition (mm. 24–32) as an interpolation between the db² in the right hand of m. 23, and the same pitch in m. 32. The db² then falls to c¹ in m. 35, providing yet another restatement of the half-step motive, as illustrated in Ex. 1.

[24] The significance of the secondary theme in the structure of this coda is explored in Joseph Kerman, 'Notes on Beethoven's Codas', in Beethoven Studies, iii. 141–59.

The first phase of this transformation begins as early as mm. 41–2, where an unexpected rhythmic deceleration, heightened dynamics, the introduction of the Neapolitan chord, and the shift to the minor mode are all conspicuous gestures that work to subvert the balance and composure of the theme. The destabilization process continues in the development, where Beethoven dramatically alters S from a variety of standpoints. The theme begins in a higher tessitura and is intensified by a steady rise in register, as the bass climbs by step for two octaves (mm. 109–23). Modulation through an incomplete sequence of descending thirds (Db–bb–Gb(= F♯)–b–c) is co-ordinated with increasing dynamic stress and thematic fragmentation (see mm. 119–22, where the last two notes of the first phrase detach and repeat three times in succession).

The theme recovers some equilibrium in the recapitulation (mm. 175–88), where it returns in the tonic major, but this becomes a point of departure for the final transformation, which takes place in the coda. Here S recurs three times. The first statement (mm. 211–17) begins in the key of 'furthest remove' from the development, D flat major, and ends in the tonic minor. Beethoven varies both the melody and the accompaniment by placing them in a still higher register and thinning out the texture, so that the melody remains monolinear until the final measures. Moreover, he redefines the phrase structure, allowing the first two measures to repeat; a subsequent acceleration in the phrase rhythm of the right hand generates a sense of quickening pulse. Beethoven's treatment of the theme here includes a further registral ascent, *sf* accents on the four rising cadences, and a climactic disruption of the texture that spills over into an explosive cadenza (Ex. 2).

After the cadenza S returns firmly grounded in the tonic minor and in a faster tempo 'più Allegro' (mm. 240–8)). The melody is reshaped to include the Neapolitan degree, Gb, finally resolved as V_9^0/iv. Moreover, the cadences outline a dramatic fall rather than a rise (a variant already emphasized in the development, mm. 119–22), and the harmonic rhythm is complicated by syncopation (see mm. 244 and 247, where the V_5^6/iv resolves to the subdominant on the weak, second beat of the measure). To emphasize further this structural landmark, Beethoven adds a new spacing of the melody and the accompaniment: the left hand descends to the bass while the right hand remains in the higher register; by the end of the presentation the distance between the two has polarized (mm. 245–8). Finally, for the first time, the theme cadences in the tonic (m. 249). The metamorphosis is completed at the close of the movement, where the opening notes of S emerge one last

Ex. 2. Phrase rhythm of *S*, first movement (mm. 210–17)

time (m. 257).[25] As if to remind us of its original shape and character, the theme begins normally on the third degree of F minor, soaring to f^3, before recoiling to merge with the final presentation of *P*. Already melodically distorted, *S* is now texturally altered, its distinctive broken-chord accompaniment displaced by the nervous tremolo previously associated exclusively with *P*.

One final point should be made about Beethoven's treatment of form in this movement. Although he clearly maintains the integrity of the sonata-form sections, he also strives for a sense of continuity. To a large extent, this continuity derives from the gradual absorption of *S* into the dark world of *P*, as we have just outlined; but Beethoven employs two other tactics to activate a sense of flow. One involves his treatment of the main articulation points, softening each pivotal juncture of the form. At the border between the exposition and the development, for example, the opening theme returns in its original

[25] The fragment in mm. 257–8 refers to *S*, because we have just heard this theme beginning on the same notes ($ab'-c^2-f^2$) in mm. 239–40. At the same time, these pitches are also part of *P*, allowing Beethoven to allude to both themes in a single gesture.

octave texture to link the two sections. Later, changes in rhythm and harmony bind the end of the development to the opening of the recapitulation: the eighth-note pedal on the dominant closing the retransition overlaps with the return, and the primary theme now enters in a six–four position, making the harmonic rhythm at the articulation point seem static. Finally, Beethoven elides the border between the recapitulation and the coda, where the low F in m. 204 functions simultaneously as the last note of the preceding section and the first note of the section to come.

The second strategy is harmonic. Beethoven incorporates large areas of dominant preparation, which interject pockets of suspense.[26] Sustained pedal-points appear at the end of the primary theme (mm. 9–16), in most of the transition (mm. 24–34), in the tail of the secondary theme (mm. 44–50), in the development (mm. 93–109), the retransition (mm. 132–5), the recapitulation (mm. 136–51), and the coda (mm. 231–8).

One of the remarkable aspects of this movement is how many large-scale features find expression on local levels. The balanced shape of the movement as a whole, for example, is reflected in two facets of the exposition's structure. The first is proportional: each thematic building block is notably similar in size. The primary theme (P, mm. 1–16) is sixteen measures long; the transition area (PT, mm. 17–23, and T, mm. 24–34) comes to eighteen measures; the secondary theme (S, mm. 35–50) is again sixteen measures; and the closing area (1K, mm. 51–60, and 2K, mm. 61–5) is fifteen measures. Secondly, Beethoven arranges his material so that selected elements from the opening of the sonata recur, intensified, at the close of the exposition.[27] Because this symmetrically constructed frame encloses thematic ideas of a highly passionate nature, there is a constant pull between constraint and freedom, generating tension for the whole section (see Table 2).

Throughout the exposition Beethoven supports this underlying pull by creating recurrent waves of tension and release. This process of ebb and flow begins with the first theme, where a highly charged atmosphere of unpredictability replaces the expected one of tonal stability. If we trace the profile of later themes, we can see how Beethoven builds to an explosive climax in the closing area. The counter-statement (PT), for example, again behaves erratically. After

[26] See Steven Lubin, 'Techniques for the Analysis of Development in Middle-Period Beethoven', Ph.D. dissertation (New York University, 1974), fo. 129. Lubin notes that 'extended passages of dominant preparation–seven bars or longer–occupy 29% of the movement'.

[27] Symmetrical aspects of the exposition are discussed in Charles Rosen, The Classical Style (New York, 1971), 400.

TABLE 2. *Symmetrical aspects of the first movement, exposition*

mm. *1–2*	Low tessitura; *pp* dynamic; *Pax* motive; octave texture; two-octave distance between the hands; root of the tonic in the lowest register of the piano (m. 1).
mm. 14–16	High–Low tessitura (melodic peak bb³, m. 14); *f* dynamic; *Pb* motive (mm. 15–16); sixteenth-note arpeggio patterning; half cadence before *PT* (m. 16).
mm. 59–60	High tessitura (melodic peak cb⁴, m. 60); *ff* dynamic; *Pb* motive, left hand, recto in m. 59, inversion in m. 60, and also implied in peak notes, cb⁴–bb³ in right hand, m. 60; sixteenth-note arpeggio and scalar patterning; half-cadence before *2K* (m. 60).
mm. 64–5	Low tessitura in left hand; (*p*)–*dim–pp* dynamics; augmentation of *Pax* in left hand; textural intensification with addition of tremolo accompaniment; five-octave distance between the hands; root of the new tonic (Ab) in the lowest register of the piano.

initially restoring calm, it erupts into an ever greater concentration of energy, introducing syncopation, massive texture, and fast textural rhythm. The rapid changes from eight-part chords to monolinear or three-part textures are shocking in their juxtaposition. Moreover, at the close of this section Beethoven treats the modulation to the secondary key in an unusual way. The new tonality, A flat, enters 'too soon', as the result of an abrupt harmonic ellipsis (Ex. 3).

Ex. 3. Harmonic ellipsis in *T*, first movement

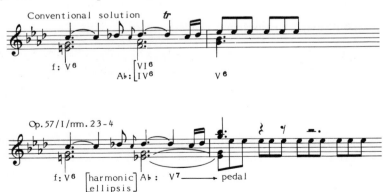

In the transition that follows harmonic motion is temporarily suspended, although local rhythmic and melodic activity continues, creating a stable plateau. The sense of relative calm is reinforced by the reduction in textural thickness and dynamic level. Accents stress the appearance of the half-step motive on Fb–Eb, now rhythmicized as a 'sigh motive'. The end of the transition, however, once again surprises: the Cb in mm. 25–30 prepares for a theme to follow in minor, but instead the secondary theme opens in A flat major.

The undermining of expectations continues in the course of the secondary theme: what begins as a conventional lyric interlude soon departs from any established norm. The dramatic augmentation in the repeated second phrase of the theme gradually dissolves into trills (mm. 44–6), while, simultaneously, textural and dynamic strength dwindle (mm. 45–50). Because the exposition will reach a peak in the next section, Beethoven further weights the approach to the climax by prolonging the dominant harmony for seven measures (mm. 44–50). This attenuates the anacrusis to the emphatic down-beat in m. 51, so that arrival in the closing area triggers a sense of release from tension accumulated throughout the exposition.

In the beginning of the closing section (*1K*) phrase repetitions and symmetry of phrase structure (4 + 4 + 2, mm. 51–60) work to contain the violent outburst. The concluding theme (*2K*) once again alleviates the tension. The left hand descends, the overall dynamic level returns to 'piano', and rests aerate the percussive sixteenth-note accompaniment in the right hand. In the penultimate measure Beethoven complicates the rhythm with subtle shifts in the contour-patterning of this accompaniment, which, when combined with the sustained notes in the bass, yield a hemiola effect (Ex. 4). The resolution of the rhythmic dissonance in m. 65, together with the expansion generated by the four-and-a-half-octave span between the hands, generate energy that drives across the articulation point into the development.

Ex. 4. Contour-patterning, first movement, mm. 64–5

The sequence of thematic events in the development closely parallels that found in the exposition. In order to facilitate the sketch discussions, I have divided this section into five parts, on the basis of thematic content.

Part A (mm. 67–78) begins with *Pax* material in the key of F flat (= E), the flat submediant of A flat minor.[28] Subsequently, a series of cadential phrases based on *Pay* (mm. 69–78) affirm this new key. Part B (mm. 79–92) combines a mutant of *Pax*, in which the original octave leap is replaced by repeated notes, with an expanded version of the tremolo accompaniment from *2K*. In three modulating phrases Beethoven exploits registral extremes, as the two hands cross in dialogue fashion.[29] The keys traversed here continue to outline the series of major thirds begun at the close of the exposition: A flat minor (m. 65), E major (m. 67), E minor (m. 78), C minor (m. 81), and finally A flat major, which now functions as the dominant of D flat major (mm. 91–2).[30] Here again, rhythmic fluctuations in the accompaniment generate momentum. Beginning in m. 81, the sixteenth-note arpeggios are grouped irregularly, so that units of five notes expand to six before each point of modulation.

Part C (mm. 93–108) consists of *T* material in D flat. Newly situated between two sections that display frequent modulation, the theme seems more stable. Beethoven adds fresh colour and provides emotional relief by using the major mode, rendering the 'sigh motives' (mm. 96–7 and 100–1) less 'pathetic'. Further variety results from the increased amount of registral contrast (note the octave leaps in the right hand in mm. 94–5, 98–9, 102, which invert the leaps from mm. 28–9). An extension based on *P* (*N*, mm. 105–8) adds the only conspicuous touch of imitation in the movement.[31]

Part D (mm. 109–22) develops *S*, building to the main climax of the development (see the discussion of this section above, p. 18).

[28] The Ab changes to G♯ in m. 65, and moves by common-tone modulation to E major.

[29] In m. 87 the right hand extends up to c^4, while the left hand plays a low Ab. William Newman has pointed out that a piano with a full six-octave range was available to Beethoven by 1803, although he did not take full advantage of it until 1807, for the piano transcription of Op. 61. See his 'Beethoven's Piano versus his Piano Ideals', *Journal of the American Musicological Society*, 23 (1970), 484–504. While the sonatas prior to 1803 use a five-octave range of less, the remaining sonatas gradually extend the range to as much as f^4 Richard Kramer has found evidence suggesting Beethoven was occasionally writing for an upper range or c^4 prior to Op. 57. See his 'On the Dating of Two Aspects in Beethoven's Notation for Piano', in Rudolf Klein (ed.), *Beethoven-Kolloquium Vienna 1977* (Kassel, 1978), 160–2.

[30] This modulatory plan produces yet another recurrence of the motive in inner voices, on Eb–E♮–Eb, as part of the chords A flat minor, E major, and C minor. See Edward Aldwell and Carl Schachter, *Harmony and Voice Leading* (2nd edn., New York, 1989), 572.

[31] Schenker ('Beethoven: Sonata Opus 57', p. 10) suggests this theme is composed of a series of descending third progressions; however, I think the neighbour-tone motion is more compelling a basis for thematic derivation here.

Part E (mm. 123–34) functions as the retransition.[32] At the outset, it continues the climax: the rise to the melodic peak (mm. 125–6) is strengthened by the harmonic disorientation resulting from the prolonged diminished-seventh chord, the fortissimo, and the sustained pedal. To counteract the melodic descent in mm. 126–9, Beethoven increases the surface rhythm in the right hand (mm. 130–5), and enriches the texture by recalling the rhythm of the *Pb* motive on Db, intensified by octave skips in the left hand. Release finally comes with the melodic expression of this motive (m. 132) and a clear dominant pedal.

At the opening of the recapitulation, *P* returns in a new, more strident setting. The percussive dominant pedal encloses the theme in a strait-jacket, filling in all the gaps originally produced by rests. It also creates syncopation and increases motivic saturation, since the half-step motion in the bass (C–Db, m. 139; B♮–C, mm. 143–4) echoes the *Pb* motive. Additional power results from the omission of any ritard or *pp* indications (compare m. 147 with m. 12). As a balance to the modulation from F minor to A flat major/minor in the exposition, the counter-statement of the theme returns in F major.[33] Because this modal change requires the addition of four measures, the prevalence of dominant harmony and loud dynamics in the primary-theme area intensifies. The remainder of the recapitulation closely parallels the exposition.

Beethoven shapes the coda, like the exposition, so that the proportions and disposition of materials are complementary. The section can be divided into six parts, on the basis of thematic content: Part A, mm. 204–10; Part B, mm. 210–17; Part C, mm. 218–39; Part D, mm. 239–48; Part E, mm. 249–56; and Part F, mm. 257–62. Parts A and F incorporate the same texture (a motive from the primary theme paired with a tremolo accompaniment) and are similar in length; Parts B and D focus on the transformation of the second theme. The result is a generalized bow-form, with the cadenza-like Part C in the centre of the curve (see Fig. 1).[34]

Harmonically, Part A offers a momentary deflection away from the tonic to D flat major. Here Beethoven integrates with an earlier

---

[32] For a discussion of this retransition, see Beth Shamgar, 'Dramatic Devices in the Retransition of Beethoven's Piano Sonatas', *Israel Studies in Musicology*, 2 (1980), 70–1.

[33] A similar key plan occurs in Op. 30 No. 2/I: in the exposition, *P* is in C minor, *S* and *K* in E flat major; in the recapitulation *S* returns in C major, and *K* in the tonic minor. Op. 67/I offers a variant of this plan, in that both *S* and *K* return in C major in the recapitulation, with the tonic minor only restored in the coda.

[34] This observation is made in Uhde, *Beethoven Klaviermusik*, iii. 200.

Part C. 21mm.
(cadenza)

Part B. 7mm.   Part D. 9mm.
(*S*)   (*S*)

Part E. 8mm.
(*NK*)

Part A. 7mm.   Part F. 6mm.
(*Pax*/tremolo)   (*Pax*/tremolo)

Fig. 1. Bow form of the coda, first movement

procedure, since the relationship between F minor and D flat major
(i–VI) mirrors the modulation from A flat minor to F flat (= E) major
at the beginning of the development. The tonal detour creates a
'whiplash' effect, making subsequent stabilization of the home key
seem even more compulsory.[35]

Part C, which is based on figuration from the retransition, constitutes the main climax of the movement. Beethoven's co-ordination
of resources here include changes in dynamics, tempo, register,
melodic shape, and harmonic rhythm. Nine measures of broken
chords concur with a more-than-two-octave rise in the bass and an
acceleration in the harmonic rhythm (mm. 218–26). The subsequent
shift to curving arpeggios (mm. 227–34) brings a deceleration in
harmonic rhythm and a rise to the melodic peak, c^4 (m. 231). Arrival
on the dominant is prolonged until the half-step motive returns,
accompanied by a reduction in dynamic level and tempo. The cumulative effect of all these gestures is a gradual quickening in pace,
followed by a broadening-out that sets the climactic resolution of the
motive (mm. 238–9) in bold relief (Ex. 5).[36]

The concluding sections both integrate and stabilize. The new
cadential theme that constitutes Part E (*NK*) unifies: although melodically derived from the primary theme, its thick texture and
irregular rhythm recall aspects of the counter-statement, *PT*. Varied
repetition serves to ground the theme here, while metric displacement
propels the action forward. Strong *sf* accents appearing on the weak
beats (mm. 249–50 and 252–3) are out of phase with the harmonic

[35] On this type of harmonic effect, see Ratner, *Classic Music*, pp. 230–1.

[36] For a similar effect in the coda of an earlier piano sonata, see Op. 10 No. 3/II/
mm. 67–72, where a steady rise in the bass, co-ordinated with a quickening of the
harmonic rhythm, leads to a recall of the new theme from the development in a high
register, analogous to the return of *S* in Op. 57/I/m. 210.

Ex. 5. Harmonic rhythm, first movement, mm. 218–39

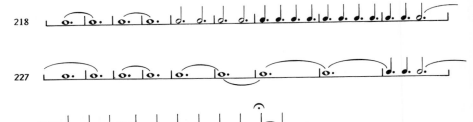

Symbols from LaRue, *Guidelines*, p.64:

Root change: ♩♩
Sustained harmony: ♪♩
Ornamental chord change: ♩♩

rhythm, which changes on the strong beats. Resolution of this rhythmic dissonance in mm. 251 and 254 reminds us of the similarly vigorous effect at the close of the exposition.[37] Tonal and rhythmic stabilization continue in Part F, and yet the metamorphosis of *S* and its total submersion in the dark world of the primary theme work at cross purposes, generating a sense of brooding unease that will only be dispelled by the hymn-like calm of the second movement.

[37] In the autograph Beethoven wrote triplet slurs over the groupings in mm. 251 and 254–5, although the 12/8 meter makes this notational clarification superfluous. In a personal communication William Newman has suggested that perhaps Beethoven did this for pianistic reasons: the slurs over the groups of three eighths are reminders that the ternary groupings still hold during the alternation of hands. Newman contrasts this effect with the opening of the finale of the 'Emperor' Concerto, where Beethoven deliberately shifts from ternary to duple groupings (see Op. 73/III/mm. 1–8).

2. Second Movement

The second movement presents one of Beethoven's best-known variation sets for the piano. The peaceful theme—with its warm, major-mode colour, even rhythmic flow, symmetrical construction, and restrained harmonies—transforms the stormy mood of the first movement into one of exalted serenity.[1]

Beethoven's choice of D flat major as tonic for this movement links it with the previous one, where this key forms crucial tonal nodes in both the development and coda.[2] Its use also balances, on an inter-movement level, the internal third relationship projected there between the primary and secondary themes (F minor–A flat major/minor), as D flat is a third below the central tonic.

The melodic profile of the theme further integrates, as the rising and falling whole steps opening the theme (Ab–Bb–Ab) can be interpreted as an unfolding of the neighbour-tone motive permeating both outer movements.[3] Differently treated, however, the motive assumes another guise: the thick texture and rich warmth of the low register coalesce to create a 'grand and elevated' effect.[4]

The theme, in binary form, consists of two eight-measure periods, each of which repeats. The harmonic plan emphasizes simple tonic–subdominant, or tonic–dominant relationships, with suspensions for colour (in mm. 3 and 7). Beethoven's spare use of dissonance, the frequent and exclusively tonic cadences, as well as the sustained inner pedal on Ab in the second period, reinforce tonal solidity. Because of the restricted harmonic palette, the German-sixth chord in m. 6 creates a vivid impact. Furthermore, the half-step relationship between

[1] Beethoven's predilection for themes relying on a song or hymn-like style becomes more prevalent in his late period. The variation movements of Opp. 110 and 111 are cases in point. See William Meredith, 'The Sources for Beethoven's Piano Sonata in E Major, Opus 109', Ph.D. dissertation (University of North Carolina, 1985), fos. 444–6.

[2] Beethoven's other minor-key works in the period up to 1808 also using the submediant for the second movement include: Op. 10 No. 1, Op. 13, Op. 30 No. 2, Op. 31 No. 2, Op. 47, Op. 67.

[3] A thorough discussion of how this motive penetrates the theme is found in Schenker, 'Beethoven: Sonata Opus 57', pp. 14–16; also see Uhde, *Beethovens Klaviermusik*, iii. 214–25.

[4] See Czerny, *On the Proper Performance*, p. 59.

the bass note of this chord and that of the subsequent dominant (Bbb–Ab) recalls a striking articulation in the development section of the first movement, where the same pitches (although not the same harmony) function as a restatement of the half-step motive (I/mm. 91–2).[5]

Beethoven has designed the movement as a miniature set of division variations, but he moulds this traditionally additive form into a dramatic structure, combining the expected accelerations in surface rhythm with a gradual rise in register.[6] As in the outer movements, the main climax occurs towards the end, at the close of Var. 3 (m. 79). Beethoven's tactics here include the rise to the melodic peak (bb[3]), the fastest surface rhythm (thirty-second notes), and the most powerful dynamics (ff in the right hand, f in the left).

Progressive developments in other stylistic elements reinforce a sense of purposive motion towards this goal. The first of these is texture. In general, there is a progressive thinning-out of the texture: from the four-part chorale setting of the theme, to the three-against-one texture caused by the rhythmic displacement of the accompaniment in Var. 1, to the essentially two-part texture in the first period of Var. 2.[7] In the second period of this latter variation Beethoven again thickens the musical fabric with a recurrence of the inner pedal on Ab. Var. 3, as the point of greatest intensification, incorporates both the most complex and the simplest textures. This is a double variation: the repeat of each half of the theme is varied (A, A[1], B, B[1]), with the two hands exchanging parts in the repeats. There is a suggestion of double counterpoint here, although the inversion is primarily rhythmic because the thirty-second notes are substantially altered in order to infuse the accompaniment with an independent melodic line. At the close of Part B (mm. 69–70) Beethoven introduces a new counter-melody in the soprano. In B[1] (beginning in m. 73) he further compli-cates the texture by blending a trill with a melodic line in the right hand.[8] The textural fabric at the principal climax, which is in five parts

[5] At one time Beethoven considered the German-sixth chord appropriate for mm. 91–2 in the first movement as well. See the discussion of the sketches for this passage below, ch. 6.

[6] A useful overview of this movement appears in Rosen, *The Classical Style*, pp. 438–9. Some other works from the middle period incorporating variation movements based on the principle of rhythmic acceleration are Opp. 61, 67, and 74.

[7] As observed in Ratner, *Classic Music*, p. 257.

[8] This is one of several examples in which Beethoven uses a special trill. In the third movement of Op. 81a, mm. 53–4, the trill and melodic line are realized simultaneously. Here, they are realized alternately, by allowing each melody note to replace one note of the trill. See William S. Newman, 'The Performance of Beethoven's Trills', *Journal of the American Musicological Society*, 29 (1976), 459–60.

as a result of the thick punctuating chords in mm. 78–9, stands in stark contrast to the naked, monolinear cadences found in other parts of the variation (mm. 52, 64, 72, and 80).

A second source of momentum resides in the steady increase of syncopation.[9] In the theme, normal metrical accents and principal melodic notes coincide. In Var. 1 the left-hand part is uniformly displaced by half a beat, acting as a rhythmic counterpoint to the main melody. Further displacement occurs when the expected melodic peak, ab′, is delayed until the third tone of the up-beat (compare m. 30 with m. 15, where the peak occurs on the down-beat). The subsequent melodic extension to bb′ (m. 31) anticipates the prominence of this same pitch, in a higher register, at the main climax point of the set (m. 79).

Beginning with Var. 2, syncopation penetrates the fabric more regularly. The main melodic line in the right hand now falls not only on the down-beat, but also on the second or fourth tones of the up-beat. The harmonic rhythm of the accompaniment is also affected; in m. 36 emphasis shifts from the tonic note, Db, to the passing tone, Eb (this is anticipated in the second ending of Var. 1, m. 32b).

In the first half of Var. 3 Beethoven uses syncopation to create a polyphonic effect. The whole-step motive of the theme is displaced by half a beat and stressed by *sf* accents, while, simultaneously, a secondary melody embedded in the accompanying figuration acts as a counterpoint. In Part A the secondary melody works to anticipate the main motive (mm. 49–50, 53–4); in A[1] it functions as an echo, extending the displacement to the second tone of the second thirty-second–note unit (mm. 57–8, 61–2).[10] At the climax Beethoven gradually realigns these elements: in m. 79 the melodic notes (in the bass of the left hand) are pulled back to the second half of each beat, and finally, in m. 80, fall on the down-beat.

The various connective techniques Beethoven employs between variations also contribute to the directional force. Throughout the cycle he forges continuity in two principal ways: dynamically, by beginning and ending each variation softly; and structurally, by progressively expanding the range and complicating the rhythm of the main cadences. At the close of the theme, for example, a falling fifth in the left hand (Ab–Db) supplies the linear tie to Var. 1. Tension is heightened at the end of this first variation by delaying arrival of the tonic note in the left hand (m. 32b). In Var. 2 the cadences

---

[9] The growth of syncopation is mentioned in Schenker's analysis and in Rosen, *The Classical Style*, p. 438.

[10] As pointed out in Sandra P. Rosenblum, *Performance Practices in Classic Piano Music* (Bloomington, 1988), 97–8.

for the first period extend the range from a fifth to a tenth (m. 40a), and finally to an octave (m. 40b); the close of the second period anticipates the thirty-second-note rhythm characterizing Var. 3. Such local events pave the way for the sweeping descent in mm. 79–80 that blurs the polarization of tonic and dominant harmonies and flows seamlessly into the final variation.

Var. 4 both recapitulates the original setting of the theme and recalls the 'exploration of musical space'[11] taking place in previous variations. Segments of the theme appear in contrasting registers, creating a hocket-like effect. At the climax the original leap of an octave (mm. 13–14) expands to two octaves (mm. 93–4), highlighted by a return of the rinforzando from m. 14. A sense of impending closure is signalled by the absence of repeats.[12]

The ties binding individual variations culminate in the link to the finale, where, in place of the expected tonic close, Beethoven re-harmonizes the soprano note, db^2, with the same suspensive diminished-seventh chord that heralds moments of tension in the first movement. The sustained harmony sounds twice: first *pp* and 'arpeggiando' in both hands, as if surveying the tranquillity of the immediate past, and again *ff* and 'secco' in the right hand, as if anticipating the tempest that is yet to come.[13] The harmonic weld forged between the two movements is strengthened by the 'attacca' indication and the loud dynamic. While resolution of this harmony is withheld until m. 20 of the finale, a trumpet-like fanfare forms a tempo bridge (III/ mm. 1–20). With a gradual acceleration from the half-notes ending the Andante to the sixteenths of the finale, Beethoven spans the emotional distance to the last movement.

[11] This phrase is taken from Ratner, *Classic Music*, p. 257.

[12] A return of the theme without repeats to close the cycle also marks the variation movement of the late Piano Sonata, Op. 109.

[13] The 'secco' appears neither in the first edition, nor in the editions of Simrock (1807), Kuhnel (1812), and Moscheles (entered at Stationers Hall, 12 Apr. 1837); but it is restored in the modern editions of Schenker and Henle-Wallner. For this interpretation of the 'arpeggiando' and 'secco' articulations, see Miriam Sheer, 'The Role of Dynamics in Beethoven's Instrumental Works', Ph.D. dissertation (Bar-Ilan University, 1989), i. 197.

3. Third Movement

Perhaps Beethoven (who was ever fond of representing natural scenes) imagined to himself the waves of the sea in a stormy night, whilst cries of distress are heard from afar:—such an image may always furnish the player with a suitable idea for the proper performance of this great musical picture. . . .

Carl Czerny[1]

Many analysts have observed that the first and last movements of the 'Appassionata' are closely affiliated.[2] The intricate network of associations Beethoven has stitched between them serves a dual purpose. On the one hand, it binds them together as members of the same family, thereby integrating the sonata on the broadest level. On the other hand, it provides an opportunity for the composer to demonstrate his powers of invention; in spite of many shared melodic, harmonic, and structural features, each movement projects a distinctly individual personality.

From the sketches we learn that ideas initially attached to the coda of the first movement were later refashioned to fit the close of the finale. Thus it seems reasonable to suggest that, from an early stage in the compositional process, Beethoven conceived of the two movements as complementary. The following remarks explore their relationship, identifying what is similar and what is unique to each.

Our search for common threads begins with overall proportions. Like the first movement, dimensions in the finale are carefully balanced so that three large divisions of the form are nearly equal in length (the exposition, 98 mm.; the development, 94 mm.; and the recapitulation 96 mm.). Furthermore, the rhythmic acceleration opening the finale is matched by a gradual deceleration of rhythmic values in the retransition. This written-out ritardando (mm. 176–211) breaks the movement

---

[1] Czerny, *On the Proper Performance*, p. 60.

[2] I am indebted to the comparisons of the two outer movements found in Uhde, *Beethovens Klaviermusik*, iii. 189–214, and in Walter Riezler, *Beethoven*, trans. G. D. H. Pidcock (New York, 1972), 166. For more details on motivic relationships, see Schenker, 'Beethoven: Sonata Opus 57', pp. 17–21, and Réti, *Thematic Patterns*, pp. 115–26.

almost exactly at the midpoint, creating a kind of symmetrical reci-
procity.[3]

Harmonic relationships form another strand of connection. The
emphasis on third-related keys, for example, is also found in the
finale, where there is a mirroring of the tonic by upper and lower
thirds. F minor, the tonic key, is flanked on the one side by the key of
the slow movement, D flat major, and on the other side by a brief
excursion in the coda to A flat major, so that Beethoven closes
the sonata with an echo of the same third relationship that marked
its opening. This allows him simultaneously to integrate and to
differentiate: whereas, in the first movement, motion from F minor to
A flat major is an open gesture leading to development and subsequent
modulations, in the finale A flat turns back to F minor almost
immediately.[4]

Other important key areas in the finale are touched on in the first
movement. C minor, which is used for the secondary and closing
areas and the end of the development, has previously appeared in the
development of the first movement (I/mm. 81–4); and B flat minor,
which opens the development in the finale, has coloured the transformation of S in the coda of the first movement (I/mm. 243–7). The
only other significant key from the first movement, D flat major, is
understandably avoided as having already saturated the ear in the
Andante.

Both movements show a mutual preoccupation with the Neapolitan
progression. In the finale, as in the first movement, this progression
(now in first inversion) shapes the primary theme and exerts influence
on future events. The second theme, for example, opens with a bII_6–i
progression in C minor (m. 76), and the same harmonic relationship
appears frequently in the development (in B flat minor, mm. 130–1,
138–9; in F minor, mm. 160–1). Beethoven also uses this chord
to preface the tempo deceleration in the retransition of the finale
(m. 176), much as the same harmony initiated the climax in the coda of
the first movement (I/m. 218).

Melodic affinities between the two movements are numerous. Both
primary themes begin with an arpeggiation of the tonic chord (downward from dominant to tonic in the first movement; upward from the
dominant in the finale, m. 20, and again downward on C–Ab–F, the
first pitches of each sixteenth-note group in mm. 20–1). Because in
both cases the theme repeats on the Neapolitan, the three-note motive,

[3] Uhde sees this ritardando as a corollary of the dynamic contraction and tempo
deceleration in mm. 235–8 of the first movement. See *Beethovens Klaviermusik*, iii.
208.
[4] Ibid. iii. 213.

C–Db–C, and its contraction, Db–C, act as unifying elements. Some obvious recurrences of these motives are listed below:

1. *1P* (mm. 20–7) contains the three-note form of the motive in the peak notes of the right hand on C–Db–C, and on Db–Eb–Db (analogous to *Pay* in I/mm. 3–4, 7–8).
2. *1P¹* (mm. 28–35): C–Db–C forms the apex of the melodic line in the left hand, highlighted by *sf* indications.
3. *2P* (mm. 36–49) contains an inversion of the motive in the peak notes on the right hand, on C–B♮–C (mm. 36–9); the compression of the motive appears simultaneously in the left hand in the 'sigh motives' on Ab–G (mm. 38–9); it expands to a whole step on Bb–Ab (mm. 42–3) and Eb–Db (mm. 46–7).
4. *2P¹* (mm. 50–63) repeats the two-note form of the motive in the right-hand 'sigh motives'; the left-hand accompaniment also includes an inversion of the motive on B♮–C (mm. 52–3, 62), and on E♮–F (mm. 56–7, 60).
5. *T* (mm. 64–75) and *K* (mm. 96–112) are based on *P*.
6. *S* (mm. 76–85) contains the three-note form of the motive in the right-hand accompaniment (mm. 77, 79, 81–5).
7. *KT* (mm. 112–18): a prolongation of Gb in the bass, falling to F, presents the motive in augmentation on scale degrees 6–5 in B flat minor.
8. Development, mm. 134–7: the three-note form of the motive on Bb–A♮–Bb, highlighted by overlapping imitation between the outer voices.
9. *1N* (mm. 142–57): based on the three-note form of the motive, which also appears in mirror inversion.[5]

Textural and rhythmic resemblances strengthen inter-movement relationships. If, for example, we compare the transition in the first movement (I/mm. 24–9) with *2P* in the finale (III/mm. 28–49), we see that in both instances a motoric accompaniment is paired with a melody in thirds; frequent rests break the melodic line, which begins with an up-beat and features 'sigh motives'.[6] Similarly, *2K* in the first movement (I/mm. 61–4) and the repeat of *S* in the finale (III/mm. 86–95) combine a legato melody with a broken-octave accompaniment; in each case, the octaves emphasize the same pitch, Ab. Finally, a variation of the iambic rhythmic pattern opening *P* in the first

[5] Schenker ('Beethoven: Sonata Opus 57', pp. 20–1) points out that the falling third motive from *1K* in the first movement recurs in the finale in *1N* (mm. 142–57), and *2N* (mm. 208–24); and in diminution in the close of the coda (mm. 341–51).

[6] Uhde, *Beethovens Klaviermusik*, pp. 196, 198.

movement (♪♪ ♩) recurs in the bass of *1P* in the finale (♩ 𝄽 | 𝄽 ⁷ ♪ | ♩), and in the accompaniment of *2P* (♩ ⁷ ♪ | ♩ ⁷ ♪ | ♩).

Additional features in common deserve mention. Both movements are in sonata form and begin with the primary theme in a low register, at a soft dynamic level; both use primary-theme material in the transition and interlock the transitional and secondary themes. They each make a dramatic entrance to the development (by simultaneously thinning the texture and lowering the dynamic level), and the recapitulation (by prolonging the identical diminished-seventh chord). In addition, long codas terminating in a tempo acceleration mark each movement. A specific allusion to the 'più Allegro' of the first movement (I/m. 238) may even be implied in the 'sempre più Allegro' before the 'Presto' of the coda (III/m. 304b), so that the final stretto seems a natural outgrowth of all that has gone before. Lastly, both movements incorporate extended areas of dominant preparation to sustain tension (III/mm. 13–19, 68–71, 118–26, 168–75, 206–11, and 300–8b; for the first movement, see Chapter 1 above), as well as elisions to further continuity between individual functions in the exposition, and between major divisions of the sonata form.

Against what is similar, there are crucial differences in the way Beethoven treats his material. Perhaps the most pronounced distinction relates to rhythm. In the finale the abrupt contrasts of the first movement are pressed into a single mood, driven by force of the propulsive sixteenth-notes established in the introduction and maintained until the coda. Even there, the march-like theme in A flat major offers little relief, since the eighth-notes of the melody proceed at such a rapid tempo.

Rhythmic homogeneity is reinforced by modal uniformity. The only respite from the dark hue of the minor occurs with six measures of A flat major in the coda. Indeed, the long development is remarkable for its slow rate of modulation; the subdominant minor established at the beginning of the section is sustained for over thirty measures.[7]

Homogeneity in rhythm and mode preclude strong thematic contrast; thus, nearly all the themes seem to derive from the primary one. In the case of the transition and the closing themes the connection is obvious, since the turn figure from mm. 20–1 informs all three functions. With the secondary theme the correlation results from a shared focus on the Neapolitan, and the inclusion of a melodic line in the accompaniment

---

[7] Uhde, *Beethovens Klaviermusik*, p. 207.

that recalls a passage in the bass from $1P$ (compare the left hand in mm. 76–7 with that in mm. 25–7).[8]

As if to compensate for the uniformity in other parameters, Beethoven enriches the texture by use of counterpoint. There is quasi-canonic imitation at the octave in the closing theme (mm. 96–7, 100–1), imitation at the beginning of the development (mm. 122–5), and, later, a mirror effect between melody and accompaniment (mm. 142–57). In comparison, the first movement contains relatively little imitation.

Yet another difference concerns Beethoven's treatment of phrase structure. Unlike the flexible, sometimes disjunctive phrases found in parts of the first movement, themes in the finale are more consistently symmetrical. Four-measure units are frequently the basis of construction; some themes add a two-measure extension to articulate the cadence (see $2P$ and S in Table 3), while the closing theme takes the opposite tack: a sustained contraction of phrase length, before a broadening-out for the link to the development.

TABLE 3. *Phrase structure, first and third movements, compared (mm.)*

P	(mm. 1–16)	$4 + 4 + 2 + 2 + 1 + 3$	$1P$	(mm. 20–7)	$4(2 + 2) + 4$
PT	(mm. 17–23)	$3 + 2 + 2$	$1P'$	(mm. 28–35)	$4(2 + 2) + 4$
T	(mm. 24–34)	$4 + 4 + 3$	$2P$	(mm. 36–49)	$4 + 4 + 6$
S	(mm. 35–46)	$1 + 4 + 4 + 3$	$2P'$	(mm. 50–63)	$4 + 4 + 6$
ST	(mm. 47–50)	4	T	(mm. 64–75)	$4 + 4 + 4$
$1K$	(mm. 51–60)	$4 + 4 + 2$	$S + S'$	(mm. 76–95)	$4 + 4 + 2 \times 2$
$2K$	(mm. 61–5)	$1 + 1 + 1 + 2$	K	(mm. 96–117)	$4 + 4 + 2 + 2 + 2 + 2 + 6$

Themes in the finale are also more squared-off: tonic endings delineate both $1P$ and $2P$, and even the transition closes in the tonic of the second key area. Although the second theme finishes on the dominant (m. 85), its repetition terminates on the tonic (m. 96) in a double-period structure. Only the closing theme employs an open articulation, sustaining the dominant ninth of B flat minor as a bridge to the development.

Two structural aspects further differentiate the movements. The first concerns Beethoven's treatment of the retransition. The same diminished-seventh chord signals this event in both movements; but, whereas in the first case the rhythm generates an acceleration towards a climax on the dominant, in the finale there is a deceleration in both surface rhythm and harmonic rhythm, so that arrival on the dominant

---

[8] Both Schenker ('Beethoven: Sonata Opus 57') and Uhde (*Beethovens Klaviermusik*) point this out.

(III/m. 205) presents a point of maximum quiescence rather than a peak of excitement.[9]

The second issue relates to Beethoven's handling of the form. In the finale the more repetitive sonata–rondo format impinges on the sonata-form design, creating a kind of hybrid. This impression partially results from the symmetrically constructed themes, as outlined above. But additional rondo-like features contribute, including the frequent reappearance of P material, the unusual repeat of both development and recapitulation,[10] the incorporation of a new theme at the beginning of the coda ($2N$), and the shaping of this theme as a closed, binary structure (see Fig. 2, which suggests how this movement might be outlined in rondo form).[11]

	Exposition		Development		Recapitulation		Coda	
Rondo sections	A	B	A C		A	B	D	A
Functions	1P, 1P¹, 2P, 2P¹	T, S, K	‖: 1P 1N K RT	1P¹, 1P², 2P, 2P¹		T, S, K :‖	2N — 1P	
Key	f	c	bb bb; bb–f				f–Ab–f	

FIG. 2. Third movement outlined as a sonata-rondo

[9] The use of a broadened time-scale, as well as emphasis on pure sound to create a sub-climax in the retransition, also occurs in Op. 55/I, Op. 60/I, and Op. 67/I (although each is worked out differently). See Bathia Churgin's comments in Churgin and Joachim Braun, *A Report Concerning the Authentic Performance of Beethoven's Fourth Symphony, Op. 60* (Research Project of the Beethoven Seminar at Bar-Ilan University, 1976–7; Ramat Gan, 1977), 9.

[10] This repeat reflects Beethoven's experimentation with means of enlarging formal proportions during this period. Of many possible examples, one might mention the final version of Op. 59 No. 2/I, where both halves of the movement are repeated. The autograph score of Op. 59 No. 1/I shows that originally Beethoven contemplated a repeat of both the development and recapitulation there. See Alan Tyson, 'The "Razumovsky" Quartets: Some Aspects of the Sources', in *Beethoven Studies*, iii. 132. From the sketches for Op. 53/I we also learn that Beethoven considered a repeat of the development and recapitulation there. See Barry Cooper, 'The Evolution of the First Movement of Beethoven's "Waldstein" Sonata', *Music and Letters*, 58 (1977), 170–91.

[11] See Malcolm Cole, 'Rondo', in *The New Grove Dictionary of Music and Musicians*, ed. Stanley Sadie (London, 1980), xvi. 175. Cole outlines a typical Beethoven rondo finale, noting that, in a minor-key movement, the first episode (analogous to S) can be in either the dominant or the relative major. In Op. 57/III S is in the dominant minor; however, the first return of the refrain (analogous to the beginning of the development) is a tonal surprise in rondo terms, because it is in the subdominant minor rather than the tonic, thereby anticipating the key of the second episode (analogous here to $1N$). The presence of a new theme in the coda is also typical. See Cole's 'Techniques of Surprise in the Sonata-Rondo of Beethoven', *Studia musicologica*, 12 (1970), 261, where Cole notes that Beethoven liked to use this procedure in the rondo finales of his piano concertos.

Finally, Beethoven shapes the concluding *Affekt* of each movement differently, so that the end of the finale counterbalances the sense of defeat or hopelessness implied at the close of the first movement. In both cases, material from the primary theme returns, together with a melodic descent (in the finale, both hands descend; in the first movement, only the left hand does). But in the first movement Beethoven fortifies the melodic drop by creating a sharp deceleration in the surface rhythm of the left hand, and a steep dynamic fall (from *ff*, m. 257, to *ppp*, m. 262). In contrast, the finale sustains the loud dynamic and steadily contracts the phrase units, so that an acceleration results (Ex. 6). Thus, despite the broadening out in the final measures, the momentum generated by this quickening of the pulse pushes beyond the final articulation, lending the tragic mood a defiant ring.

Ex. 6. Contraction of phrase length, third movement, mm. 341–61

PART II.   THE SOURCE OF
THE SKETCHES

4. The Sketchbook Mendelssohn 15

All the known and accessible sketches for the 'Appassionata' are found in the largest of Beethoven's sketchbooks, Mendelssohn 15.[1] Also called the *Leonore* sketchbook, the major part of this volume is devoted to the 1805 version of Beethoven's opera (revised in 1806, and again in 1814, when it was retitled *Fidelio*); but, in addition to Op. 57, ideas also appear for the song 'An die Hoffnung', Op. 32; the Piano Sonata in F major, Op. 54; the Triple Concerto, Op. 56; and the String Quartet, Op. 59 No. 1.[2]

Alan Tyson has made a comprehensive study of this sketchbook, and his conclusions, together with my own examination of the manuscript, form the basis for the following remarks.[3] More recently, Theodore Albrecht has suggested a new chronology for the first two hundred pages.[4] Since his arguments have a direct bearing on dating the Op. 57 sketches, they will be briefly summarized at the end of this chapter.

The history of Mendelssohn 15 has been carefully traced by Tyson. After Beethoven's death the sketchbook was sold at the Nachlass auction of 5 November 1827 to the music publisher Artaria and Company. On 14 June 1834 it was purchased by the Berlin collector

[1] An additional leaf with sketches for Op. 57 is mentioned by Otto Albrecht as Census 231C in his 'Beethoven Autographs in the United States', in Kurt Dorfmüller (ed.), *Beiträge zur Beethoven Bibliographie: Studien und Materialien zum Werkverzeichnis von Kinsky-Halm* (Munich, 1978), 3. Albrecht reports that this leaf was sold in 1964 to an unidentified collector. I have been unable to trace its present location, and apparently no known photograph of it exists.

[2] The contents of the sketchbook are detailed in Hans-Günter Klein, *Ludwig van Beethoven: Autographe und Abschriften* (Staatsbibliothek Preussischer Kulturbesitz: Kataloge der Musikabteilung, i/2; Berlin, 1975), 231–77.

[3] 3. Alan Tyson, 'Das Leonoreskizzenbuch (Mendelssohn 15): Probleme der Rekonstrucktion und der Chronologie', *Beethoven Jahrbuch*, ix (1977), 469–99. The original English version of this essay appears in Stephen Spector (ed.), *Essays in Paper Analysis* (Washington DC, 1987), 168–90. See also Tyson's summary, 'Mendelssohn 15', in Douglas Johnson, Alan Tyson, and Robert Winter, *The Beethoven Sketchbooks: History, Reconstruction, Inventory* (Berkeley and Oxford, 1985), 146–55. I am grateful to Dr Tyson for sending me the original English text before its publication.

[4] Theodore Albrecht, 'Beethoven's *Leonore*: A New Compositional Chronology', *Journal of Musicology*, 7 (1989), 165–90.

Heinrich Beer; the first page of the manuscript still carries Artaria's seal and this date. The manuscript subsequently passed to Paul Mendelssohn-Bartholdy, and then to his son Ernst. On 26 June 1908 it was given to the Royal Library in Berlin. Currently, the sketchbook forms part of the Paul and Ernst von Mendelssohn-Bartholdy Stiftung in the Staatsbibliothek Preussischer Kulturbesitz in West Berlin.[5]

The sketchbook is still enclosed in the brown cover of Heinrich Beer's library. It contains 173 leaves (or 346 pages) of sixteen-stave oblong paper, all with the same watermark of a shield with three six-pointed stars under a crown, and the letters VG.[6] The overall structure of the book is quite regular: each gathering is made from a single large sheet that was folded and cut to form two bifolia; these were then placed one inside the other to create four leaves, or eight sides, and then sewn together. There are, however, several places where these 'single-sheet' gatherings are either incomplete or irregular, indicating that the present format of the manuscript in some way differs from what it was when Beethoven laid it aside. A considerable portion of Tyson's investigation seeks to restore an accurate picture of the book's original structure. He examines descriptions of the source by earlier scholars, studies the continuity of sketches, and applies other modern techniques of physical analysis, such as matching ink-blots on facing pages, noting watermark–quadrant succession, and identifying remnants of missing leaves.[7]

As Tyson notes, earlier scholars who examined the manuscript included Otto Jahn (in 1863), Alexander Wheelock Thayer (in 1872), and Gustav Nottebohm (before 1879). Because Nottebohm's discussion is the most thorough, Tyson analyses it in detail.[8]

With regard to the structure of the book, Tyson accepts Nottebohm's conclusion that pp. 23–6 of the manuscript should precede p. 1.[9] His supporting evidence involves three factors: musical content (these pages contain sketches for the Prisoner's Chorus, part of the finale to

[5] On the history of the Mendelssohn collection, see Johnson, Tyson, and Winter, *The Beethoven Sketchbooks*, pp. 37–9.

[6] See ibid. 549 for an illustration of this paper-type, which is classified as number 17.

[7] The original size of Mendelssohn 15 is not known, but Tyson demonstrates that it has suffered considerable damage. For a complete review of the reconstruction techniques applied, see ibid. 44–67.

[8] Tyson establishes that Nottebohm's account of the manuscript was probably written before 1879, although it was not published until later. See Gustav Nottebohm, 'Ein Skizzenbuch aus dem Jahre 1804', in *Zweite Beethoveniana* (Leipzig, 1887; repr. New York, 1970), 409–59 (hereafter abbreviated as *N II*).

[9] This rearrangement must have occurred before Beer bought the book, because Artaria's seal with the date of Beer's purchase appears on p. 1. See Tyson, 'Das Leonoreskizzenbuch', p. 481.

Act II of *Leonore*), sketch continuity (an entry on p. 22/sts. 6 and 7 is continued directly on to p. 27), and physical analysis (there is an ink offset from p. 22/st. 2 to p. 27/st. 2). Nottebohm's claim that a page is missing between p. 26 and p. 1 is shown to be incorrect, however, because an ink-blot connection links these two pages. Noting that pp. 23–6 form an incomplete gathering, Tyson has further identified the missing bifolium as pp. 43–6 of the miscellany Landsberg 12.

More importantly, Nottebohm's assumption that pp. 183–6 and 199–202 are interpolations is also confirmed. Tyson's arguments here are especially pertinent, because in both instances the leaves in question interrupt sketches for Op. 57, which appear on pp. 182, 187–98, and 203. In the case of pp. 183–6 (which contain sketches for the last three movements of Op. 59 No. 1), the presumed misplacement can be corroborated by two physical factors: ink-blots on p. 182 have produced offsets on p. 187; and an ink stain on the outside edge of staves 12 and 13 links pp. 179–82 with pp. 187–98, skipping over pp. 183–6.

Regarding pp. 199–202, however, the evidence of interpolation is unfortunately less definitive. Tyson's analysis of the watermarks on these pages reveals a leaf is missing after p. 198; he points out that, if we were to suppose that pp. 199–202 are in fact correctly placed, 'we should in that case have to assume that there had once been a further bifolium, now lost, enclosing pp. 199–202. Thus, the jarring transition from p. 198 to p. 199 could have been softened by the contents of two (lost) leaves.'[10] In spite of admitting this possibility, Tyson believes that pp. 199–202 are wrongly placed, and his argument relies on musical content: the sketches on these pages are for the Triple Concerto, Op. 56, and, as Tyson points out, the compositional phase found here for the second movement seems regressive when compared to sketches for the same movement found earlier in the manuscript, on p. 140. If Tyson's conclusions about this part of the manuscript are correct, it could mean that, with the exception of the leaf missing after p. 198, the sketches for Op. 57 originally continued in an unbroken sequence from pp. 182 to pp. 203.

Tyson also agrees with Nottebohm that the last four leaves (pp. 339–46) are extraneous to the original sketchbook and, accordingly, he terminates the integral manuscript with sketches for the *Leonore* Overture, No. 2, on p. 338. The first performance of *Leonore* took place on 20 November 1805, so he suggests that Beethoven would have finished sketching in Mendelssohn 15 around the end of October.

Tyson next addresses the question as to whether Mendelssohn 15 originally consisted of one unusually large sketchbook or of two

[10] Tyson, 'Das Leonoreskizzenbuch', p. 482. The quotation is from the English version of this article.

smaller ones. He notes that the descriptions offered by both Thayer and Nottebohm specify a pair of volumes rather than the single one we see today, and that this view is also inferrable from Jahn's account of the book.[11] For purposes of reconstruction, therefore, Tyson provisionally accepts a bipartite conception, because, as he observes, in the period 1801–8 it was Beethoven's general habit to work with sketchbooks of ninety-six leaves. This is about half the size of Mendelssohn 15, so the present length could have resulted from merging two similar sketchbooks of the 'normal' length.

Unfortunately, neither Thayer nor Nottebohm gives any clue as to where the break between the two books occurred; nor does any conclusive physical evidence survive. Tyson begins his search for a likely point of division with two assumptions: each book would have consisted of not more than ninety-six leaves; and the break could only have occurred between pages that do not display any physical linkage by ink-blot or offsets. Given these preconditions, he suggests the following as potential nominees: pp. 164, 168, 174, and 180. Sketch continuity between pp. 164 and 165 makes this site unlikely, and a marginal ink-blot on the edges of pp. 170–82 unites these pages, eliminating p. 180 as a possibility. Of the two remaining candidates, p. 168 seems the more satisfactory, because it is left blank, and is followed by a gap of three missing leaves. Noting that the outer portions of a sketchbook would be the most vulnerable to damage, Tyson hypothetically divides the manuscript after p. 168, at the place where two of the three missing leaves would intervene. Book I would thus have initially contained twenty-four, four-leaf gatherings, twenty-two of which remain; Book II, which was originally the same size, now consists of twenty-two gatherings and the beginning of a twenty-third. (For the complete reconstruction, see Tyson's diagram of the sketchbook in *The Beethoven Sketchbooks*, pp. 152–5.)

Having established a probable time when Beethoven gave up using the sketchbook, Tyson concentrates on two additional chronological issues: when did Beethoven actually begin work in Mendelssohn 15; and does the inscription on p. 291, dated 'am 2ten Juni' in Beethoven's hand, originate in 1804, as Nottebohm maintains, or in 1805?[12] Marshalling the evidence surrounding the genesis of *Leonore*, Tyson posits a date of June or July 1804 for the beginning of the sketchbook.[13]

[11] Tyson, 'Das Leonoreskizzenbuch', p. 472.

[12] The full remark, in translation, reads: 'On 2nd June–finale always simpler—all piano music likewise—God knows—why my piano music still always makes the worst impression on me, especially when it is badly played.'

[13] The complex web of information brought to bear on this conclusion involves a discussion of sketches for *Vestas Feuer* and earlier sketches for *Leonore* found in

With regard to the second issue, Tyson argues that the comment on p. 291 dates from 1805. His reasoning hinges on the dating of the sketches for 'An die Hoffnung', Op. 32, which appear on pp. 151–7 of the sketchbook. Tyson points out that, in a letter from Countess Josephine Deym to her mother, dated 24 March 1805, Josephine states that Beethoven had presented her with a manuscript of this song as a gift. Several earlier letters written by Josephine's family in January 1805 mention that Beethoven had completed 'an air pour Pepi' (one of Josephine's nicknames). Tyson believes that this 'air' was 'An die Hoffnung', and that Beethoven might even have given it to Josephine as a New Year's present; thus he conjectures that the sketches for it would probably date from some time in December 1804. If so, it seems more likely that the remark written later in the book, on p. 291, springs from June 1805 and not from 1804.[14]

Using Tyson's valuable detective work as a point of departure, we can now explore the possibilities for dating the 'Appassionata' sketches. As noted above, these sketches begin on p. 182, at a point between the two inner areas of the manuscript dated by Tyson. Thus, they can tentatively be assigned to the months January–June 1805. This hypothesis must, however, be correlated with other external evidence relating to the sonata's history. First, we must take into account the famous description by Ferdinand Ries of Beethoven working at the piano on an idea for the finale of Op. 57:

Once we were taking a similar walk in which we went so far astray that we did not get back to Döbling, where Beethoven lived, until nearly 8 o'clock. He had been all the time humming and sometimes howling, always up and down, without singing any definite notes. In answer to my question what it was he said: 'A theme for the last movement of the sonata has occurred to me' (in F minor Op. 57). When we entered the room he ran to the pianoforte without taking off his hat. I took a seat in the corner and he soon forgot all about me. Now he stormed for at least an hour with the beautiful finale of the sonata. Finally he got up, was surprised still to see me and said: 'I cannot give you a lesson today, I must do some more work.'[15]

The general assumption in the literature has been that this event took place during the summer of 1804.

Landsberg 6 and in a group of ten additional sketch leaves. See Tyson, 'Das Leonoreskizzenbuch', pp. 486–91, and *The Beethoven Sketchbooks*, p. 149.

[14] See Tyson, 'Das Leonoreskizzenbuch', pp. 491–4, and *The Beethoven Sketchbooks*, p. 150.

[15] Franz Wegeler and Ferdinand Ries, *Biographische Notizen über Ludwig van Beethoven* (Coblenz, 1838; facsimile edn., Hildesheim, 1972), 99; Eng. translation from *Thayer's Life of Beethoven*, rev. and ed. Elliot Forbes (Princeton, 1964; repr. 1970), 356.

Secondly, there is Beethoven's letter to the publisher Breitkopf & Härtel, dated 26 August 1804, listing three piano sonatas among a large group of works being offered to them, including the 'Eroica' Symphony, Op. 55, the Triple Concerto, Op. 56, and the oratorio *Christus am Oelberge*, Op. 85. Beethoven did not specify any details about the sonatas, but it is assumed he was referring to the 'Waldstein' Sonata, Op. 53, the F major Sonata, Op. 54, and the 'Appassionata', Op. 57.[16] Both Op. 53, which is sketched in Landsberg 6, and Op. 54, the second movement of which occupies parts of pp. 8–14 and 18–21 of Mendelssohn 15, could have been ready, or nearly so, by late August; but, if we accept Tyson's dating of the later portion of the manuscript, the Op. 57 sketches would only have been entered in the book after the date of this letter. Of course it is possible that, with two sonatas in a fairly finished state, Beethoven was projecting the speedy completion of the third. He might have already formed a clear concept of the work in his mind, and even have made some preliminary sketches for parts of it. This latter speculation is supported by an early finale sketch on p. 191/sts. 1–2, which only faintly resembles the final version, suggesting the sketch may have been copied out from an earlier idea.

Beethoven sent two subsequent letters to Breitkopf & Härtel that we can relate to the genesis of Op. 57. The first, written 16 January 1805, reports that, while Opp. 53, 54, and the 'Eroica' had already been sent, delivery of the third sonata (probably Op. 57) had been delayed, due to the illness of his preferred copyist.[17] This date approaches the tentative one suggested above for the inception of the Op. 57 sketches. However, even though it is known that Beethoven could work very quickly,[18] many of the sketches seem too early for Beethoven to be writing that the sonata was ready to go to the copyist.

The last letter, dated 18 April 1805, reports that Beethoven would be sending them 'the two works which I still intended you to have' (Opp. 56 and 57) within four to six weeks.[19] In fact, negotiations with this firm ultimately broke down and all of these compositions, with the exception of Op. 85, were eventually published in Vienna by the Bureau des Arts et d'Industrie. But the letter offers us a probable

---

[16] Anderson No. 96.

[17] Anderson No. 108. Alan Tyson has suggested this copyist was Schlemmer, who worked regularly for Beethoven during 1804–5. See Tyson, 'Notes on Five of Beethoven's Copyists', *Journal of the American Musicological Society*, 23 (1970), 442.

[18] Alan Tyson's discussion of a Sketchbook of 1810–11 in *The Beethoven Sketchbooks*, pp. 201–6, suggests that Beethoven worked rapidly on Opp. 117 and 113, sketching about twenty-two leaves in a period of three weeks, or about one leaf a day.

[19] Anderson No. 111.

terminus ante quem for the 'Appassionata' sketches of late April or early May 1805.

The question remains as to when Beethoven actually began the Op. 57 sketches in Mendelssohn 15. Here the evidence is less conclusive. As Tyson has shown elsewhere, we cannot entirely trust Ries's dating of his memories.[20] There are many small inaccuracies in Ries's biographical material, which was written towards the end of his life, more than thirty years after many of the events he described.[21] Furthermore, the final version of the sonata emerged long after August 1804 (the paper of the autograph dates from 1806 and the sonata was published in February 1809), so Ries could have heard Beethoven play a finale for the sonata at some later time, perhaps in 1805.[22] With regard to Beethoven's first two letters to Breitkopf & Härtel described above, we must remember that Beethoven sometimes exaggerated the readiness of his works to publishers, so that could be the case here.

As noted above, Theodore Albrecht has proposed a new compositional chronology for the part of the sketchbook containing the 'Appassionata' sketches. While it is not my purpose to present a formal criticism of all his arguments, I will review a few relevant points. Taking the August 1804 date as the only reasonable one for Ries's story, Albrecht maintains that not only the finale sketches for Op. 57, but all the other surviving sketches as well, were written 'some time during the first three-and-a-half weeks in August 1804'.[23] Regarding the sketches for 'An die Hoffnung', Albrecht speculates that Josephine's depression after the death of her husband in January 1804, coupled with her growing feelings for Beethoven in the early summer of 1804, were the catalyst for Beethoven's composition of this song. He thus thinks the likely date for these sketches would have been not December but June 1804, when Beethoven was staying in Hetzendorf, before moving to Baden on 6 July.[24] In this interpretation Josephine's March 1805 letter to her mother can be viewed as a belated revelation of Beethoven's

---

[20] See Alan Tyson, 'Ferdinand Ries (1784–1838): The History of his Contribution to Beethoven Biography', *19th-Century Music*, 7 (1984), 216–17.

[21] e.g., on p. 77 of Wegeler and Ries, *Biographische Notizen über Ludwig van Beethoven*, Ries reports that 'In the year 1802 Beethoven composed at Heiligenstadt his Third Symphony (now known as the *Sinfonia eroica*).' But, as we now know, Beethoven wrote the third symphony in 1803, not 1802, and he wrote it at Baden and at Oberdobling, not at Heiligenstadt.

[22] Ries does not date this incident. But it is possible that it occurred just before he left Vienna in September 1805.

[23] Albrecht, 'Beethoven's *Leonore*', pp. 167–8, 187.

[24] Ibid. 168–9; Josephine was also in Hetzendorf at this time.

gift, with the delay attributable to her unease regarding the increasing intensity of their relationship.

Albrecht's conclusions also assume that more than 150 pages of Mendelssohn 15 would have been sketched by late June, and in order to accommodate this amount of work, he suggests Beethoven began using the sketchbook perhaps as early as 1 May. His reasoning here involves the sketches for Op. 56 found on pp. 14–17, 96–7, and 132–42, all of which were probably written before early June 1804.[25]

Albrecht further proposes that the two interpolations occurring in the midst of the 'Appassionata' sketches also originated before August 1804: that pp. 183–6, containing sketches for the String Quartet, Op. 59 No. 1, could have been written during the end of July 1804 when Beethoven was in Baden;[26] and that pp. 199–202, containing additional sketches for Op. 56, could have been completed before the reading of this work undertaken with Lobkowitz's orchestra in late May or early June 1804.[27]

The problem with Albrecht's method is that at many points he relies too heavily on speculation. In particular, we might point to his conjectures that Josephine's psychological depression in June 1804 prompted Beethoven to sketch 'An die Hoffnung' for her; that Beethoven would consciously place the sketches on pp. 183–6 for Op. 59 No. 1 between two consecutive pages with sketches for Op. 57 as 'a reminder to himself where the quartet fit chronologically in his creative process';[28] and that, with regard to pp. 199–202, Beethoven 'could have easily have left an extraneous double leaf in the book almost absentmindedly'.[29]

When evaluating evidence dealing with issues of chronology, we must also emphasize that, while it is thought Beethoven generally used the pages of a sketchbook more or less in order, it is equally clear he sometimes moved forwards and backwards within a book as new ideas for a work in progress occurred to him, or simply to use up empty space.[30] Thus it is possible that, after mapping out whole

---

[25] There are several articles dealing with the evidence that Op. 56 was copied out for a trial performance that occurred in late May or early June. See Reinhold Brinkmann, *Österreichische Musikzeitung*, 12 (1984), 636; Tomislav Volek and Jaroslav Macek, 'Beethoven's Rehearsals at the Lobkowitz's', *Musical Times*, 127 (1986), 78; and Jana Fojtíková and Tomislav Volek, 'Die Beethoveniana der Lobkowitz-Musiksammlung und ihre Kopisten', in *Beethoven und Böhmen* (Bonn, 1988), 228.

[26] Albrecht, 'Beethoven's *Leonore*', pp. 176–7.

[27] Ibid. 177–8 n. 39.   [28] Ibid. 177.   [29] Ibid. 178.

[30] That spatially adjacent sketches are not necessarily chronologically adjacent was first pointed out by Alan Tyson in 'The 1803 Version of Beethoven's *Christus am Oelberge*', *Musical Quarterly*, 56 (1970), 570–1. See also Rachel W. Wade, 'Beethoven's Eroica Sketchbook', *Fontis artis musicae*, 24 (1977), 254–89. As Wade notes, 'one can

portions of the sketchbook for work on *Leonore*, he could have jumped ahead to jot down an idea for Op. 57, subsequently turned back to empty pages to work on 'An die Hoffnung', and later gone forwards to the Op. 57 pages as new ideas occurred to him.

It would seem, therefore, that we can only say with certainty that Beethoven was probably working on the sonata in late 1804 and early 1805, and that Ries might have heard him play a version of the finale in August 1804; but it could just as easily have been another piece he heard, or it could have been a misdating of the event. Even if Ries did hear a version of the finale in 1804, this does not mean that all the other sketches were entered at the same time. Finally, Beethoven's April 1805 letter to Breitkopf & Härtel suggests that the surviving sketches were completed by late April or early May 1805. As the following discussion of the sketches will show, however, there must have been additional work on the sonata, at least for the second and third movements, that is now lost to us, so we must assume that we have only part of the compositional story.

hardly escape the conclusion that Beethoven did not always fill the book in an orderly fashion, page by page . . . if there can be three or more layers of activity represented on a single page, it is no longer possible to assume that a given sketch dates from the same time as others "around" it' (p. 269).

PART III.   THE SKETCHES

5. Overview and First Movement: Exposition

Sketches for all movements of the 'Appassionata' appear on fourteen pages in the second half of Mendelssohn 15 (pp. 182, 187–198, and 203). Their visual impact reflects Ries's description of Beethoven in the grip of creative intensity (see above, Chapter 4). Ideas for different sections of a movement, or even for all three movements, can occur in quick succession on a single page; often there are dense areas of revision, and connective signs linking alternatives for a specific passage frequently interrupt the flow of a sketch.

Not all parts of the sonata are represented equally. Ideas for the second and third movements are relatively sparse, and limited in scope: sketches for the Andante concentrate on achieving a satisfactory sequence for the variation set, while work on the finale is confined to the opening tempo bridge. None the less, even these few entries prove valuable for the clues they furnish concerning Beethoven's priorities at this early stage.

Fortunately, the sketches for the first movement offer a rich opportunity for study. In them we find several long drafts for each of three major sections—the exposition, the development, and the coda—and many shorter sketches for specific themes, phrases, and even harmonic ideas. Especially provocative is a series of entries for an imitative motive, apparently intended to fit into the coda, but ultimately rejected as unsuitable.

The following detailed inventory of the sketches is organized by function. Where possible, I have placed the sketches in a suggested chronological order. The abbreviations for functions are described above, in Chapter 1. If a sketch of some length includes at least two thematic functions, it is referred to as a 'continuity draft' (abbreviated here as CD).[1]

---

[1] The term 'continuity draft' is first used in Lewis Lockwood, 'On Beethoven's Sketches and Autographs: Some Problems of Definition and Interpretation', *Acta musicologia*, 42 (1970), 32–47. I am using the term as defined by Bathia Churgin in 'Beethoven's Sketches for his String Quintet Op. 29', in Edward H. Roesner and

*Inventory of the Sketches for Op. 57**

MOVEMENT I

Exposition (mm.1–65)

CD I	182/sts.11–16
CD II	192/sts.1–10 to 193/sts.1–2 (includes the beginning of the development)
CD III	190/sts.7–11a
P (mm.1–16)	182/sts.2–3 to st.6; 182/sts.4–5; 182/sts.11–12a (CD I); 182/st.10; 187/sts.4/5a; 187/st.6b; 189/st.9; 187/st.16; 192/sts.1–4 (CD II)
PT (mm.17–23)	182/sts.12b–13a (CD I); 188/sts.11a/12a; 192/sts.5–6a (CD II); 203/sts.3/4(?); possibly related sketches: 189/sts.7/8; 189/st.11; 198/sts.11/12 (intended for use in the coda?)
T (mm.24–34)	182/st.13b (CD I); 182/st.9; 192/sts.6b–7 (CD II); 188/st.10(?)
S (mm.35–50)	187/sts.5b–10b; 187/st.6a; 189/sts.12/13; 189/sts.14–15a; 193/sts.9b–10; 192/st.11 (CD II); 197/sts.9/10; 190/st.15
1K (mm.51–60)	182/st.14 (CD I); 192/sts.8–9a (CD II); 190/sts.7–9a (CD III)
2K (mm.61–5)	182/sts.15–16a (CD I); 187/st.15; 188/st.12b; 192/sts.9c–10 (CD II); 190/sts.9b–10 (CD III)
Another alternative for the closing area	193/sts.11–12a(?)

Development (mm.66–134)

CD	194/st.5–14
Possible Draft	203/sts.6–11
Part A (mm.66–78)	182/st.16b; 187/st.7; 187/st.8; 187/st.9; 188/st.8a; 187/st.4b; 192/st.10b to 193/sts.1–2; 190/st.11a; 193/st.5; 194/st.5; 193/sts.14–15; 195/st.3

Eugene K. Wolf (eds.), *Studies in Musical Sources and Style: Essays in Honor of Jan LaRue* (Madison, Wisconsin, 1990), p. 450, n. 35.

Part B (mm. 79–92)   194/sts. 5b–7 (CD); 196/sts. 1–5; 190/st. 13c;
                            196/sts. 6–8/9; 196/sts. 11–12;
                            203/sts. 6–10(?); 190/sts. 13a; 193/sts. 6/7;
                            203/st. 1

Part C (mm. 93–108)   194/sts. 8–10a (CD); 194/sts. 15/16 (for N?)

Part D (mm. 109–22)   193/st. 13; 194/sts. 10b–12 (CD); 193/st. 16;
                            198/st. 10

Part E (mm. 123–35)   194/sts. 12–14 (CD); 203/sts. 11–15(?)

Recapitulation (mm. 135–204)

P   196/st. 15a

PT   197/st. 3/4b

T for mm. 162–6   193/st. 3b
    for mm. 167–8   192/st. 12

Coda (mm. 204–62)

CD I   192/sts. 13–16

CD II   195/sts. 10–15 to st. 1/2

CD III   197/sts. 14–16

CD IV   198/sts. 4–8

Related sketches: 187/sts. 11–12; 188/st. 6; 188.sts. 8/9b;
                            193/st. 8; 194/sts. 1–3; 196/sts. 15b–16;
                            197/sts. 1–2; 197/sts. 8a, 8b; 190/sts. 11b–12b;
                            198/sts. 14–15

Sketches which may be   193/st. 4c; 195/st. 8a; 197/st. 3a; 197/st. 12;
either for the cadenza-   198/st. 9
like Part C of the coda
or for similar figuration
in the retransition

Imitative motive   187/st. 13; 188/st. 15; 189/st. 10; 190/st. 7b;
                            192/st. 14b (CD I for the coda); 195/st. 12b
                            (CD II for the coda); 197/st. 7; 197/st. 11b
                            (from p. 198/st. 14?)

Sketches where func-   182/st. 7 (PT in E?); 188/st. 14 (S ?);
tion is ambiguous: 190/st. 9b; 190/st. 12a; 193/st. 7b; 195/st. 4a

MOVEMENT II

Var. 1   190/st. 1(?); 190/st. 2a; 190/st. 5b; 191/st. 4a

Var. 2   190/st. 2b (words only); 191/st. 6a

Var. 3	190/sts. 2c/3c; 190/st. 4a; 190/st. 5c; 191/st. 6b
Link with finale:	191/st. 4b
'Concept' sketch:	195/sts. 4b–6b

MOVEMENT III

Preliminary idea	191/sts. 1–2
Introduction	191/sts. 4c–5; 191/sts. 8/9–11a; 195/sts. 6a/7

SKETCHES TRANSCRIBED BY NOTTEBOHM
(in *N II* 437–41)

Movement I	182/sts. 2–6; sts. 11–16; 192/sts. 6–8a, 11; 190/sts. 7–9a, Imitative motive: 187/st. 13; 195/st. 12
Movement II	195/sts. 4b–6b
Movement III	191/sts. 1–2; 191/sts. 4b–5

★ In the sketch citations in the inventory and the text, the page number of the manuscript is given first, followed by the stave numbers (abbreviated as 'st.'); if a sketch is continued directly from one stave to the beginning of the next stave, those staves are connected by an en-rule; when a sketch occupies more than one stave vertically, references to these staves are connected by an oblique; the letters 'a', 'b', and 'c' are used to distinguish multiple entries appearing on a single stave, with 'a' referring to the entry farthest to the left of the stave. Thus, for example, 195/sts. 10–15 to sts. 1–2 means that a sketch begun on p. 195 stave 10 moves horizontally through stave 15 and then continues in vertical format on staves 1 and 2. Staves cited for continuity drafts include the full draft, which sometimes extends into another section of the movement. Subsequent discussions of these drafts, however, usually deal with discrete sections, omitting reference to such extensions.

As is apparent from the Inventory, the types of sketches vary considerably. Typically, the continuity drafts are flanked by shorter entries for specific themes or phrases, either emending material already found in the draft, or anticipating material that is yet to come. CD I for the exposition, for example (p. 182/sts. 11–16), is preceded by preliminary studies for the primary theme (sts. 2–6), and followed by revisions of the transition (st. 9) and the primary theme (st. 10). The material immediately subsequent to the draft (on p. 187) introduces new ideas for the second theme (sts. 5b–10b), the development (sts. 7, 8, 9), and the coda (sts. 11–12).

Among the smaller entries, a 'concept' sketch for the second movement stands out (p. 195/sts. 4b–6b); it presents a little catalogue of ideas for the variations.[2] There is also a brief harmonic plan (p. 190/st. 12a), which may have been intended to outline a passage in the coda.

In general the sketches are restricted to a single stave, but thicker textures often occur when a particular sonority is crucial. For example, the pairing of a melodic tremolo in the treble with an augmentation of a motive from *P* in the bass—the texture articulating the close of the exposition, recapitulation, and coda in the first movement—usually appears in piano score. More than one voice also appears occasionally for functions incorporating parallel thirds (such as *T* or *2K* in the first movement), or full chords (the main theme of the second movement, or the introduction to the finale). In some instances Beethoven provides an harmonic bass to clarify the voice-leading in a problematic passage; a good example occurs in the course of work on the second theme of the first movement (see p. 197/sts. 9/10).

Sometimes there are special verbal instructions. These range in scope from dynamic indications to structural pointers (see Table 4). The most surprising dynamic indication is the *cresc.–ff* in a sketch for the conclusion of the coda in the first movement, a sharp contrast to the unusual *ppp* ending in the final version. The structural pointers vary in purpose. Some, like the 'ultimo pezzo' on p. 191/st. 1, refer to the cycle as a whole; others are expressive (as, for example, the 'simplice' on p. 195/st. 6), or give formal prescriptions (for example, the 'senza repetizione' on p. 191/st. 6 and p. 195/st. 6, directing the omission of repeats for each half of the theme in the close of the second movement).

The only articulation sign is a legato slur followed by a stroke, marked over an entry for Var. 2 of the second movement. For the final version Beethoven substituted a more subtle form of syncopation, in which the irregular concurrence of metrical accentuation and melodic line—played 'sempre ligato'—creates a gentle, rubato-like effect. The more pointed style seen in the sketch was then reserved for Var. 3. The only tempo indication, the 'presto' noted over an early sketch for the coda of the first movement, was similarly shifted to a later place in the final version, where it marks the tempo acceleration in the coda of the finale.

---

[2] The term 'concept' sketch is first used in Tyson, 'The 1803 Version of Beethoven's *Christus am Oelberge*', p. 571. An instance in which this sketch-type functions at the inter-movement level is found in the Kessler Sketchbook, fo. 37ᵛ, where Beethoven writes out themes for all three movements of Op. 30 No. 1, before beginning to sketch the first movement. See *Ludwig van Beethoven, Kesslersches Skizzenbuch*, ii. *Faksimile*, ed. Sieghard Brandenburg (Bonn 1976).

TABLE 4. *Dynamics and pedal markings: Sketches and final version compared*

Page	Indication	Function	Final version
190/st.4	pp	II/mm.79–80?	ff–dimin.
191/sts.8–9	ped.	III/O	ped., mm.1–5
192/st.3	f, p	I/m.13	pp, f, mm.12–13
193/st.1	ppp	I/dev., m.66	pp, m.65 ff.
193/st.14	f	I/dev., m.71	no f; ⟨ ⟩
194/st.5	sf	I/dev., Pt.A	sf, mm.74, 77
194/st.13	f, ped.	I/dev., Pt.E	ff, ped., mm. 123 ff.
195/sts.1/2	cres., ff; con p [ed.]	I/coda, end	pp, ppp, mm.260–3; pedal included
198/st.10	pp	I/dev., m.109	p
203/st.9	ped.	I/dev.?	?

	Words written in the sketches★
190/st.2	Var. [variation]; triol[en]
190/st.4	Cd [coda?]
191/st.1	Ultimo pezzo
191/st.6;	senza repetizion[e]
192/st.15	fine
195/st.6	simplice
195/st.6	senza repetizione
195/st.13	presto
196/st.16	Cod[a]
197/st.8	bis
197/st.11	point d'orgue
203/st.11	3 mal

★ 'Vide' connections, 'etc.', and colons not included.

One idiosyncrasy of the first-movement sketches pertains to metre. While some areas are clearly written in 12/8 (such as *PT*, *1K*, and, sometimes, *2K*), others are in 4/4 (*P*, *T*, and *S*). Because this inconsistency occurs as early as CD I for the exposition and continues intermittently, sometimes emerging within a single function (see, for example, p. 192/sts. 1–10, the *P* theme), it would seem that Beethoven always intended the movement to be in 12/8, but was simply impatient with the fussy notation required for writing certain themes in this metre.[3] His choice of 12/8 here is unusual, but perhaps it was deter-

[3] For some general rhythmic peculiarities in the sketches, see Joseph Kerman (ed.), *Ludwig van Beethoven: Autograph Miscellany from circa 1786 to 1799* (the 'Kafka

mined by his conception of the tempo. In the final version he marked this movement 'Allegro assai', and the use of 12/8 rather than 4/4 ensured that a light touch and lively pace would prevail.[4]

Finally, it should be mentioned that in five instances sketches for numbers from the 1805 version of *Leonore* appear at the top of the page.[5] Beethoven probably entered these first, when he was mapping out whole portions of the sketchbook for work on the opera. In the ensuing discussions all of the sketch examples are excerpted from the complete transcriptions given in Part V. For the transcription procedures, the reader is referred to the prefatory explanations given there.

FIRST MOVEMENT: EXPOSITION

There are three continuity drafts for the exposition: two present a view of the whole, while the third focuses exclusively on the closing area. If we compare the basic structure of these drafts with the final version, it becomes apparent that, from the first, Beethoven had a clear sense of the amount of time needed for most functions (see Table 5).[6] The lengths of the primary theme, the transition, and the second closing theme are established in CD I and change little. Expansion in total length for the final version is thus largely due to the addition of the secondary theme, and amplification of the first closing area, *1K*.

CD I and Related Sketches

Before drafting the exposition, Beethoven made several preliminary sketches for *P* (p. 182/sts. 2–6). From these we learn that, while the beginning of the theme (*Pa*) and the tapping motive on the dominant (*Pbm*) were already fixed, the material linking them, as well as the

Sketchbook') (London, 1970), ii, p. xiii. Kerman notes that Beethoven was often impatient with smaller note values. With regard to the fluctuating metre, see also Sieghard Brandenburg, 'The Historical Background to the "Heiliger Dankgesang" in Beethoven's A-minor Quartet Op. 132', in *Beethoven Studies*, iii. 174. As Brandenburg notes, the sketches suggest Beethoven also had difficulty finding the appropriate metre indication for the slow tempo of this movement.

[4] On the interrelationship between choice of metre and tempo, see Rosenblum, *Performance Practices*, p. 306.

[5] Notation or verbal instructions relating to the following numbers appear: No. 18 (p. 182), No. 15 (pp. 187 and 188), No. 1 (p. 189), and No. 17 (198). The entries for *Leonore* are identified in Klein, *Ludwig van Beethoven. Autographe und Abschriften*, ii. 255–7.

[6] This is also true of the sketches for Op. 29/I, as noted by Churgin, 'Beethoven's Sketches', p. 463.

TABLE 5. *Proportions, first movement, exposition: Final version and continuity drafts compared* (mm.)

	Total length	Length of functions					
		P	PT	T	S	1K	2K
Final version	65	16	7	11	16	10	5
CD I (p.182/sts.11–16)	45*	17?	7	10	—	4	7
CD II (p.192/sts.1–11)	57	16	7	11	11	7	5
CD III (p.190/sts.7–10)	13	—	—	—	—	8	5

Note:
　Elisions not counted; dashes indicate absence of function.
　★ This number includes mm. 1–7 of P, which have been worked out above the draft on sts. 2, 4 and 5.

subsequent approach to the dominant cadence (mm. 14–16 in the final version, hereafter designated as *Pc*), were still evolving. Beethoven experimented with two different versions of *Pa*. The first outlines a sequential rise for the trills before falling to the dominant; the second reverses direction, so that the trills descend.[7] In both cases, other harmonies intervene between the Neapolitan and the dominant. We can guess Beethoven rejected these alternatives as being too diffuse for an opening gesture, because ultimately he left the progression in F minor, i–♭II–V, uncluttered. Emphasis on the dominant and its ensuing prolongation was thereby sharpened, and the whole primary theme became more directionally focused (Ex. 7).

　The draft itself begins with the second phrase group (*Pb*, mm. 9 ff. in the final version). Unfortunately, Beethoven gives no clue as to which of the two versions of the first phrase were intended to preface the draft, but the initial pitch, c^2 (st. 11) connects smoothly with a point in the second version (st. 4, m. 4). If we further assume that st. 4 continues from the opening measures of the theme presented in the first preliminary sketch on st. 2, the entire length of *P* in this draft would be seventeen measures (Ex. 8).

　While this approximates the length of the final theme, the internal proportions are different: the tapping motive falls on the fourth, rather

　[7] This initial draft also implies that the rhythm of the tapping motive (♫♩) was derived from the trills, as suggested in Schenker, 'Beethoven: Sonata Opus 57', p. 6.

Ex. 7. Early sketches for *P*

than the second, beat of the measure, requiring additional rests. Comparing the phrase structure generated by this placement with the final version, we see how Beethoven's conception of this passage grew. From a seemingly random plan, with persistent breaks in continuity, he developed a carefully graded pattern of modular halving, with a broadening-out at the cadence (Table 6).[8] He also activated the melodic line: whereas the sketch of *Pb* seems static, with the pattern e^2–f^2–e^2 sounding twice in the same register (Ex. 8), the final version of this phrase ascends.

For the third phrase, *Pc*, Beethoven captured the mobile contour of the final theme, but made the rise–fall pattern less extreme. Worth

TABLE 6. *Phrase modules in P, first movement: Final version (mm. 1–16) and continuity drafts compared (mm.)*

Final version	$4 + 4 + 2 + 2 + 1 + 3$
CD I (Ex. 8)	$4 + 2 + 3 + 3 + 1 + 4$

---

[8] The term 'modular halving' is used in Judith Schwartz, 'Opening Themes in Opera Overtures of Johann Adolf Hasse: Some Aspects of Thematic Structural Evolution in the Eighteenth Century', in Edward Clinkscale and Claire Brook (eds.), *A Musical Offering: Essays in Honor of Martin Bernstein* (New York, 1977), 247. Schwartz notes: 'Beethoven exploited the device of quickening phrase rhythm by halving modular length several times in succession, especially at moments of transition or development.'

Ex. 8. Suggested opening and CD I, *P*

noticing is the slower, half-note rhythm for the cadence, which seems lifeless when compared to the more breathless effect Beethoven would later develop here; and the melodic dip to G in the last measure, which masks the return of the half-step motive in augmentation, on Db–C (analogous to mm. 15–16 in the final version).

Beethoven later revised the theme, and his second thoughts, recorded on st. 10, are cued into the main draft by two '+' signs (Ex. 9).[9] Significant changes occur here: the tapping motive is pulled back to begin on the second beat; the final register of the trills is achieved; and the textural growth of the motive, from single notes in the bass to thirds for the reverberations in the soprano, emerges. In addition, the arpeggio beginning *Pc* rises to a higher peak, implying the more extreme registral polarization of the final passage.

Ex. 9. Revisions for *P*

[9] I am assuming st. 10 was written after st. 11, because of the way in which the final notes of st. 10 are crammed on to the end of the page.

Beethoven's first formulation of the transition area (Ex. 10*a*) comes remarkably close to the final version in terms of length, pitches, and register, but the first four measures are, with the exception of a register change, mechanically repeated, a procedure he would replace with rhythmic and melodic developments in the next draft. A later refinement on st. 9 includes the prefix for the introductory trill (Ex. 10*b*).

Ex. 10. CD I, *PT* and *T*

Surprisingly, the draft now moves directly to A flat minor for the *1K* theme. Not only is the lyrical, secondary theme absent, but there is no reference to a melody in any major key. Beethoven did not even leave space for future insertion of such an idea—something he often did when he was still unsure of the specific material he wanted to include. It would seem, therefore, that at this point he was considering an entirely different kind of exposition: something all in minor and rather monochromatic in mood, perhaps like the first movement of his earlier Piano Sonata, Op. 31 No. 2.[10]

While we cannot know Beethoven's overall strategy for the movement at this stage (i.e. what he planned to use in place of the conflict generated in the final movement between *P* and *S*), we can see that he had already decided *1K* would form the rhythmic and emotional peak of the exposition. The theme itself is distinctly recognizable, although several details mute its climactic impact (Ex. 11). The length is much

---

[10] On the later addition of the secondary theme, Donald Tovey (*A Companion to Beethoven's Pianoforte Sonatas* (London, 1935)) remarks 'the glorious afterthought converted the whole movement from the gloom of a storm to the active passions of tragedy', (p. 170).

Ex. 11. CD I, 1K

shorter; the melody is more static, because there is no change of register on the repeats; and the surface rhythm is less driving, due to the mixture of eighths and sixteenths (although continuous sixteenths may have been implicit here). Furthermore, the harmony moves from tonic to subdominant in the first subphrase (1Kx); in subsequent drafts, Beethoven would modify this to read tonic to submediant.

This first exposition draft concludes with a version of 2K in which the *Pax* motive appears twice, metrically displaced, creating a boldly skewed effect (Ex. 12). Also different is the melodic profile—a steep rise from bass to soprano, followed by a return to mid-range. Beethoven later reworked the registral plan so that a gradual descent finishes off 2K; as a result, the overall melodic contour of the exposition assumed a more pronounced archlike shape, congruent with the soft dynamics at either end.

Ex. 12. CD I, 2K

Two further details in the sketch of 2K deserve mention. In the first measure, the last note, D♮, suggests that a V^0_9/V chord was intended here. Beethoven eventually used a simpler harmony for this spot (a V^4_3 chord in m. 63), transferring the more dissonant diminished-seventh chord back to the close of 1K. Similarly, the pitches fb^2–eb^2, a transposed restatement of the half-step motive from P, were also repositioned in the next draft to the end of 1K; but their presence here alerts us to their subtle recurrence in the final theme (see mm. 61–3, the left hand, the upper notes in the second and third dotted quarters).[11]

---

[11] As Philip Gossett suggests, sketches can often 'provide us with an analytic insight about the final version that might otherwise elude us'. See his 'Beethoven's Sixth Symphony: Sketches for the First Movement', *Journal of the American Musicological Society*, 27 (1974), 263.

From the end of the draft, where Beethoven indicated an opening for the development, we learn that the choice of non-repeating sonata form was an early one, as was the idea of initiating the development with a key related by a half-step to the tonic (in this case, F sharp minor), introduced by means of an enharmonic modulation.

CD II and Related Sketches

Short studies for the exposition appearing on pp. 187–9 anticipate many of the new developments we shall observe in CD II.[12] The several sketches for the primary theme focus on the c phrase (mm. 14–16). The first (Ex. 13a) predicts a texture characteristic of the retransition and coda in the final version: arpeggiated chords divided between the hands. The harmony outlines a cadential progression, i–iv–V₇–i, culminating in an augmentation of the half-step motive on Db–C with fermata. Again, the motive is camouflaged, this time by placing the final tone, C, in an inner voice.

The remaining sketches work out this massive cadence (Ex. 13b–f). If we compare them with the final version (Ex. 13g), we realize that Beethoven's decision to stress the recall of the half-step motive became fixed only after alternative solutions had been explored first. On p. 187/st. 6, for example, he divided the pitches of the motive so that they frame intervening shorter notes. On p. 189/st. 9 he eliminated all reference to the motive, substituting instead an ascending arpeggio ending in the higher register. While Beethoven later rejected this alternative, he retained its upper border, bb³, for the peak of Pc in the final version (m. 14). A sketch on p. 187/st. 16 closely approximates the completed cadence.

In contrast to the systematic evolution traceable in sketches for P, the two brief entries for PT offer only rough ideas for characteristic aspects of this function. While texture is probed on p. 188/sts. 11a/12a, syncopation is the focus of the sketch on p. 189/sts. 7/8.

There are also two entries for 2K (Ex. 14). In the first, the six-and-a-half-measure length established in CD I is reduced to four measures, one less than the final version. The phrase structure is reorganized, so that a repeated one-measure module in parallel thirds is followed by a two-measure augmentation of the Pax motive ($2 \times 1 + 2$). Although the distribution of material now resembles the final theme, the use of musical space is less dynamic, because the theme clings to the middle register (eventually this function encompasses an expanse of nearly four octaves). In the second sketch Beethoven experimented with a

[12] Sketches appearing on these pages that relate to S are discussed below, pp. 69–74.

Ex. 13. Sketches for the cadence of *Pc* and final version compared

new second phrase, which recalls the dotted rhythm of *Pax*, sustains the parallel thirds, and descends to the lower register. Only the last feature of this alternative became an important determinant of the exposition's final shape.

CD II (see Part V, the transcription of p. 192/sts. 1–11 to p. 193/sts. 1–2) displays substantial growth in nearly every function. In the primary theme *Pa* now corresponds to the final version, but two options appear for *Pb*. Beethoven seems to have copied the first of these directly from his initial draft, as the tapping motive falls on the fourth beat. He later incorporated the revision so that the motive

Ex. 14. Sketches for *2K*

begins on the second beat, and added 'forte' and 'piano' indications. For the final version Beethoven would reverse the position of these dynamics, in order to support the swift mood changes here: he combined the softer level with a ritardando, enhancing the aura of mystery and suspense (m. 12), and placed the forte with the return to the original tempo, an expansion of range, and an increase of rhythmic excitement (m. 13).

The third phrase (*Pc*) is also closer to its final form, although it begins an octave lower. Similarly, small refinements in *PT* (the trills added on st. 6, mm. 1 and 3, and the added suffix for the trill in m. 3) suggest that Beethoven was more confident about this section, and perhaps went directly to the autograph without the need for further sketching.

In the transition area mechanical repetition is replaced by textural enrichment (thirds) and registral contrast. Although there are no further exposition sketches for *T*, ideas advanced for this theme in later parts of the movement come much closer to mm. 28–31 of the final version (see p. 194/sts. 9–10 for *T* in the development; p. 192/st. 12 for *T* in the recapitulation). It would seem, therefore, that a process of cross-fertilization may have occurred here. Even in the autograph these measures are heavily revised, and thus we can assume that Beethoven still had difficulty with them in the final phase of composition.

In the closing area *1K* is extended both vertically and horizontally. The repeat of the second subphrase (*1Ky*) now drops to the lower register, and three additional measures (*1Kz*) develop the half-step motive, in transposition (Fb–Eb) and in inversion (D♮–Eb). Beethoven used both forms in the final version (see mm. 58–9 for the transposition; m. 60 for the inversion).

Ideas culled from the intervening sketches contribute to the reformulation of *2K*. While the first phrase accords with the sketch on p. 188/st. 12b, the second phrase derives from the sketch on p. 187/

st. 15. The five-measure length of the final theme is thus achieved, although the dramatic descent to the low A♭ is yet to come.

The most significant architectural change in this draft is the interpolation of *S* (note the 'Vide' connection leading from the end of st. 7 to the beginning of st. 11); this important addition will be discussed below, together with all the other entries for this theme.

CD III

In the last exposition draft Beethoven worked to strengthen the closing area (Ex. 15). He bolstered *1K* by extending its length to eight measures, and revamped its phrase structure so as to create an overall feeling of acceleration into *2K* (see Table 7).[13] He also changed the harmony of the first subphrase (*1Kx*) to i–VI, rather than i–iv as in previous drafts. Later, Beethoven would use this new progression on a modulatory level to signal two important articulative points: the beginning of the development, which modulates from A flat minor to F flat (or E) major; and the beginning of the coda (from F minor to D flat major). In retrospect, then, this local harmonic change became an important tactic for integration.

Another integrative touch was introduced in the second subphrase (*1Ky*), where Beethoven added a reference to the Neapolitan harmony in A flat minor (written in the draft with an A♮ in the bass rather than B♭♭, as in mm. 53 and 57 of the final version). He also gave the theme greater breadth, as both subphrases now rise on the repeats,

TABLE 7. *Phrase structure of* 1K, *first movement: Final version* (mm. 51–60) *and continuity drafts compared* (mm.)

	x	*y*	*x*	*y*	*z*			
Final version (10mm.)	2	2	2★	2★	2	or	4 + 4 + 2	acceleration
CD I (4mm.)	1	1	1	1	—	or	2 + 2	static
CD II (7mm.)	1	1	1	1★	3	or	2 + 2 + 3	broadening out
CD III (8mm.)	1	2	1★	2★	2	or	3 + 3 + 2	acceleration

Note:
    ★ indicates change of register on repeat; dash indicates absence of subphrase.

[13] On this point, see *N II*, p. 440.

although the climactic ascent to the highest range of Beethoven's piano in *1Kz* does not yet appear.

The entry for *2K* appears to derive directly from the previous draft. But a later annexation of tiny notes (see p. 190/st. 9, mm. 3–4) shows that Beethoven was already contemplating an opening in the higher register (see mm. 61–2 in the final version).

Ex. 15. CD III for the exposition

The Evolution of the Secondary Theme

Before surveying the growth of *S*, it is useful to ask why Beethoven felt this theme was needed. Certainly, CD I and the original version of CD II–both of which lack it–have structural integrity. They include the necessary ingredients of primary, transitional, and closing areas and present tonal, if not modal, contrast in the F minor–A flat minor opposition of keys.[14] They outline an exposition with rhythmic

[14] Richard Kramer points out that in early sketches for Op. 30 No. 2/I the exposition shows the same key relationship, i–iii, in the context of C minor. See his 'The Sketches for Beethoven's Op. 30 Violin Sonatas: History, Transcription, Analysis' Ph.D dissertation (Princeton University 1973), ii. 337. The relevant sketches are in the Kessler Sketchbook, fo. 54ᵛ/sts. 10–11. In the final version of the violin sonata Beethoven closed the exposition in E flat major rather than minor. The key plan of the exposition in Op. 57/I combines both ideas: the transition prepares A flat minor; the second theme opens in A flat major, but turns back to the minor for the end of the exposition.

variety and a definite formal shape: from the sweep of the opening phrase, intensification builds to the excited rhythm of $1K$, with a broadening-out for the close. Why then did Beethoven insert yet another theme?

There could have been any number of reasons. Perhaps he sensed the overall dimensions of the exposition draft were too limited to support the powerful thrust of its material. The massive outburst at the end of the primary theme, or the high energy produced by $1K$, needed a more spacious environment in order to emerge with force and clarity. An expansive melody could provide the necessary breathing space (see, for example, Op. 31 No. 2/I mm. 21–40, where the transition theme serves this function). Such a theme could also offer emotional relief from the surrounding tension, and, more importantly, lay the basis for developing a relationship with the primary theme that could be made to sustain long-range continuity.

Beethoven's formation of an appropriate vehicle to accomplish all of these ends begins in five short entries between CD I and CD II (Ex. 16). At this early stage his attempts may seem remote, yet on closer inspection each sketch displays some element that found its way into the final theme.

We can see, for example, that the first sketch (Ex. 16a) has a similar melodic profile: an arpeggiated beginning, an ascent to a peak of eb^3 (close to the fb^3 in m. 46 of the final version), with a gradual descent at the close. There are also a number of rhythmic correspondences. The trochaic pattern in mm. 1–4 of the sketch ($\quad$) resembles that in the opening of the final version ($\quad$). Furthermore, the syncopation in m. 3 of the sketch pertains to mm. 37, 39, 41, and 42 of the final version, and the triple subdivision of the beat concluding the sketch has an analogue in the last four bars of the finished theme.

The trochaic rhythm persists in the second sketch (Ex. 16b), which is entirely in the minor and may therefore relate to the second phrase of the theme.

The third sketch (Ex. 16c) contains two relevant features; it begins in major and ends in minor, and it starts with a broad, stable opening on a rising tonic arpeggio. Also noteworthy is the emphasis on Fb–Eb in the last measure, as well as the fast surface rhythm in the bass, two elements that would later be incorporated into $1K$.

The fourth sketch (Ex. 16d) may present an idea for the end of the theme, as suggested by its descending profile and triplet-eighth rhythm. The harmony implied, a chain of descending thirds (C–Ab–F–Db–Bb), may even have influenced Beethoven's final plan for the beginning of the development, which progresses through keys descending in major thirds.

Ex. 16. Early sketches for *S*

In contrast to the first four sketches, which are isolated, the fifth sketch (Ex. 16*e*) is excerpted from a larger draft.[15] Like sketches 1 and 3, it opens with an arpeggio on the tonic; and, like sketches 1 and 2, it employs a trochaic rhythm pattern. Two additional details anticipate the final version: the phrase structure is parallel, with the second phrase an octave higher than the first; and the repeated Eb pedal at the close reminds us of the sustained dominant harmony underlying the third phrase in the final theme. However, the continuation of this

[15] I am grateful to Sieghard Brandenburg for helping me to transcribe this barely legible theme.

sketch (see Part V, the transcription of p. 193) diverges radically from the final conception: it is in major and derives from P, recalling the C–Db motive, and moves to C minor for the onset of the development.

Although these early sketches show Beethoven searching for contrast, they give no hint of the equally strong impetus towards thematic interrelationship.[16] In this respect, there is a quantum leap instead of a progressive line of growth, and suddenly, in sketch 6, a clear statement of the second theme emerges (Ex. 17). It is possible that the organic connection between P and S was made after Beethoven had restudied and reworked the exposition, because the sketch is appended to the second continuity draft. While it comes very close to the final theme, a comparison of the two admits of some crucial differences. In each instance, both phrases of the theme begin in parallel fashion ($a + a^1$), but only the final version transcends mechanical symmetry, introducing a remarkable rhythmic augmentation in the second phrase to highlight the modal switch from major to minor. The imbalance created by this revision generates tension and sustains momentum, propelling us beyond the confines of the self-contained melodic unit. Another similarly motivated difference is evident in the melody of the first phrase; whereas, in the sketch, this phrase descends to cadence on the tonic, in the final version it ascends to a half-cadence on the dominant. The reversal of direction creates a more open effect, driving the action onward, and paving the way for future development.

The two remaining exposition sketches for S concentrate on the second subphrase (γ) of Sa^1. Sketch 7 (Ex. 18a) captures the augmentation, but implies a different harmonic plan in which the bass moves up chromatically, outlining the progression i_6–iv–V_9^0/V–i_4^6–V in A flat minor. Ultimately, Beethoven interpolated the Neapolitan harmony

Ex. 17. CD II, S

[16] The idea of using a secondary theme that mirrors the primary one also evolved slowly in sketches for Op. 2 No. 1/I. The first draft for the exposition of this sonata (in $N\,II$, pp. 564–5) shows that originally Beethoven had a more contrasting idea in mind for S.

between the subdominant and diminished-seventh chords. This unifying touch may already be implicit in the melody of sketch 8 (Ex.
18*b*), which closely parallels the final version.

Ex. 18. Sketches for *Sa*¹

Finally, a comparison of the harmonic rhythm for this second
phrase in sketches 6–8 with that of the final theme suggests that
Beethoven was striving for a stronger deceleration effect here, to
mediate between the relaxation of *S* and the furious energy of *1K*. The
close of sketch 8 implies prolongation of the dominant marking the
final version; here Beethoven also compensates for the slowed harmonic
action by returning to the trills used to close sketch 6 (Table 8).

Unfortunately, none of the later sketches shows how the character
transformation of this theme evolved. A detail in the development
version of *S*, however, furnishes additional evidence that cross-
fertilization could effect the composing process. When Beethoven
wrote the theme in D flat major for inclusion in the development draft,
he began on the down-beat with a dotted half-note (see below, Ex.
25*b*). In contrast, the exposition version added to CD II opens with
rests, so that the secondary theme now begins like the primary one,
with an up-beat. This integrative touch was retained, and thus the
exposition version probably post-dates the development one.

TABLE 8. *Harmonic rhythm implied in sketches for part of S, first movement: Final version* (mm. 41–6) *and sketches compared*

	Measures						Length (mm.)	Type of pattern
	41	42	43	44	45	46		
Final version	𝅝.	𝅗𝅥. 𝅗𝅥͡𝅘𝅥.	𝅝. ͡	𝅝.	𝅝.	𝅝.	6	deceleration or rest–motion–rest
	I⁶	iv–bII⁶	i⁶	V	V	V		
Sketch 6 (p.192/st.11, mm.7–10)	𝅗𝅥. 𝅘𝅥	𝅘𝅥 𝅘𝅥	𝅗𝅥. 𝅘𝅥	𝅝	𝅝		5	deceleration or motion–rest
	I⁶–IV	I⁶–V⁷	bVI–i⁶	V⁰₉/V	V	—		
Sketch 7 (p.197/ sts.9–10)	𝅝	𝅝	𝅝	𝅘𝅥 𝅘𝅥			4	slight acceleration or rest– motion
	I₆	iv	V⁰₉/V	i⁶–V	—	—		
Sketch 8 (p.190/st.15)	𝅝	𝅝 (𝅘𝅥 𝅗𝅥.?)	𝅝 ͡	𝅝	𝅝 ͡	𝅝	6	deceleration or rest–motion–rest
	(I⁶)	iv (or iv–bII⁶	i⁶	V	V	V		

6. First Movement: Development, Recapitulation

Sketches for the development include only one continuity draft. Fortunately, the draft is relatively comprehensive, although certain aspects, such as the motivic fragmentation and harmonic expansion of S (mm. 117–22 in the final version), do not appear. Most of the shorter entries focus on Part B (mm. 79–92), and, because they provide a window on Beethoven's compositional concerns for this section, they will be discussed in some detail.

We begin by examining sketches for the transitional link and Part A (mm. 66–78). Beethoven's earliest attempts suggest that he planned to modulate from A flat minor to F sharp minor. Evidence for this scheme, which alludes to the Neapolitan tonality of G flat major (= F sharp major), occurs at the close of CD I for the exposition (Ex. 19a), and, again, in two entries on p. 187. The first of these (Ex. 19b) employs a motive derived from *Pax*; the harmony moves from A flat major to minor, and then points towards F sharp (the motion is through E♮, which is enharmonically VI in A flat minor).[1] The next entry (Ex. 19c) shows a more gradual connection to F sharp minor, but, like the previous sketch, emphasizes motion from E♮ to F♯. Clearly, these two pitches were already on Beethoven's mind; later, they would form the basis for a tonic-to-supertonic progression in E major (mm. 71–8 of the final version). Both sketches on p. 187 include a fermata, and, while this break in momentum was quickly dropped for this passage, we may find some vestige of it in the long rests in mm. 70 and 72 of the final version.[2]

Beethoven's subsequent decision to start the development in E major surfaces on this same page, where mm. 66–7 appear in final form (Ex. 19d). This choice of key seems similarly generated by the

---

[1] F sharp minor could be reached through an enharmonic modulation to B minor (the common tones are F♭ and C♭ in the chords, A flat minor: VI$_6$ → B minor: iv$_6$), which could then move to a dominant chord on F♯. This F sharp major chord could then become minor for the next phrase.

[2] This fermata recalls the end of *P*, m. 16.

Ex. 19. Early sketches for the development, Part A

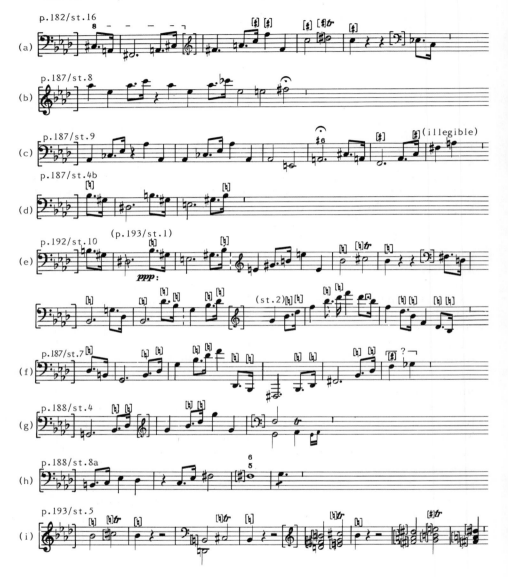

opening Neapolitan gesture of the movement, since E is a half-step below the tonic, just as Gb (= F♯) is a half-step above it.[3]

Ideas for the ensuing modulations can be gleaned from the close of CD II for the exposition (Ex. 19e). Here, Beethoven pushed past E major into B minor, and then G major; this last harmony seems to have been intended as a dominant of C minor (or major).[4] Several other fragments reiterate the same harmonies. In one case, G major precedes B minor (Ex. 19f); in another, G major is sustained while motivic action progresses from *Pax* material to the trills of *Pay* (Ex. 19g). In a third attempt, G major appears as the goal of a dominant-seventh chord in first inversion (Ex. 19h).

All of these efforts to plot a tonal course emphasize motives derived from *Pax*; but evidence that the trills from *Pay* would be equally important in Part A appears in a sketch on p. 193 (Ex. 19i). Registral contrast, another characteristic element shaping mm. 71–8 in the final version, is also anticipated here.

Beethoven now proceeded to draft the whole development. The opening measures are absent from the continuity draft, but, again, the preliminary sketches allow us to grasp not only the opening key, but also the overall proportions for each section. If we compare the length of each part of the draft with the final version, we see that the latter is only slightly longer, primarily because of expansion in Part A, although Parts C, D, and E would also be slightly extended (Table 9).

The beginning of the draft (Ex. 20) has its analogue in m. 71 of the final version. At this stage Beethoven had already absorbed the F sharp minor chord stressed in the preliminary sketches into the key of E major, where it functions as the supertonic. Perhaps he realized that deferring the sound of this chord until *after* the establishment of E major allowed him to include yet another variant of the opening gesture: minor tonic to major Neapolitan in F minor now becomes major tonic to minor supertonic in E major.

Motivically, this passage develops the trills from *Pay*. Three versions are discernible, with rhythm clearly the focus of attention, because Beethoven's revisions introduce syncopation. This syncopation seems to derive from a prominent spot in the secondary theme (m. 37 in the final version), and therefore its inclusion here, in combination with a motive from *P*, works to strengthen the bond between these two themes. The two sforzandi added in the second version were ultimately

---

[3] As suggested in Steven Lubin, 'Techniques for the Analysis of Development in Middle-Period Beethoven', Ph.D. dissertation (New York University, 1974), fo. 129.

[4] A sketch on p. 193/sts. 11–12 for what appears to be a rejected *K* idea also suggests the key of C minor for the beginning of the development.

TABLE 9. *Proportions, first movement, development: Final version (mm. 67–134) and continuity draft compared* (mm.)

	Total length	Length of parts				
		A	B	C★	D	E
Final version	68	12	14	16	14	12
CD (p. 194/sts. 5–13)	64(?)	9†	15	15	12	12(?)

★ Part C consists of functions *T* and *N*; no entry for *N* occurs in the draft, but a sketch related to it is found on the bottom right-hand corner of the page. I have not included this separate sketch in the calculations.

† In attributing nine measures to Part A, I have included the five measures for the beginning of the section that have been worked out in the preliminary sketches but are lacking in the draft.

Ex. 20. CD for the development, Part A

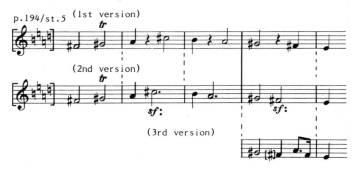

retained for the final section, where Beethoven placed them strategically to emphasize both the syncopation and the harmonic juxtaposition of the E major and F sharp minor chords.

The next portion of the draft outlines Part B (mm. 79–92). It is extremely terse, but nevertheless the basic melodic plan of this passage is plain (Ex. 21). A rising motive derived from *Pax* alternates with sixteenth-note patterning in two-measure units. Equally clear is the tonal frame, which begins with E minor, and ends with emphasis on the pitch G♯ (enharmonically the A♭ in the bass of mm. 91–2). What remains ambiguous, however, are the intervening harmonies.[5]

[5] E minor moves to A minor through its dominant, and the terminus, centring around G♯, is preceded by what seems to be a supertonic-to-dominant progression in D minor. The dominant of D minor then becomes the submediant in C sharp minor, leading to a dominant on G♯.

Ex. 21. CD for the development, Part B

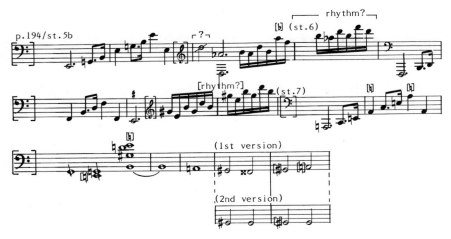

Beethoven gives two alternatives for the last measures. In one, both upper and lower neighbour-tones of the G♯ appear, anticipating the half-step vacillation between A♭ and A♮ in mm. 91–2 of the final version; in the second version the G♯ is sustained, thereby slowing both the surface rhythm and the harmonic rhythm. The psychological effect of this latter plan is contrary to the final one, where both of these elements accelerate, making this passage a climactic moment.

A linear descent from G♯ to C♯ links into the next section (Ex. 22). Beethoven later crossed out this bridge, but retained the idea of ending Part B with the rhythmic intensification implied in the motoric sixteenth-notes marking this sketch.

Ex. 22. CD for the development link into Part C

The draft for Part C (mm. 93–108) consists of a transposition to D flat major of T from CD II for the exposition, with an added preface on the dominant, A♭ (Ex. 23). Again, there is evidence that Beethoven worked over this section. Cancelled flats on st. 9 imply that at one time he intended to include modal contrast in this area: D flat major in the first phrase would become minor for the second phrase. Perhaps he reconsidered when he realized he had already used modal change for shading in Parts A and B. The end of this section makes no reference to

Ex. 23. CD for the development, Part C

the new theme in mm. 105–8 of the final version (*N*), but an isolated entry in the corner of the same page may be the forerunner of this passage; it is in the same key and moves in triplet eighths (Ex. 24).

The draft for Part D (mm. 109–22) begins like the final version, with *S* in D flat major (Ex. 25*b*). The down-beat start, however, harks back to a previous notation on p. 193 (Ex. 25*a*). The speculation posited earlier (Chapter 5), that the development version of the theme emerged before the addition of *S* to CD II for the exposition, is reinforced when we observe that the melodic presentation is remarkably similar in both sketches.[6] Here, as there, the second phrase of the theme consists of a mechanical repetition of the first, but with the modulation from D flat major to B flat minor appearing abruptly at the end. For the final version Beethoven placed the modulation earlier, so that the second phrase now seems to grow naturally out of the first. In this regard, the simultaneous change to an open articulation for the

Ex. 24. Sketch for *N* in the development

[6] Barry Cooper has observed a similar work pattern in sketches for Op. 53/I, where Beethoven first formulated the closing theme (mm. 50–7) in the context of development sketches. See his 'The Evolution of the First Movement of Beethoven's "Waldstein" Sonata', p. 178.

Ex. 25. Sketches for *S* in the development, Part D

close of the first phrase contributes to the sense of impending development.

The last segment of the draft corresponds to Part E (mm. 123–33). The proportions here are ambiguous because of the 'etc.' appearing on st. 13. Nevertheless, dynamic and pedal indications (*f*, 'ped.', st. 14) show that Beethoven regarded this as a major climax zone (Ex. 26). Aspects of this sketch bear a striking resemblance to parts of the coda in the final version: the rising bass from C to F outlined on st. 12, and the arpeggiated patterning of the diminished-seventh chord on st. 13, resemble material found in mm. 220–3; and on st. 14 the two fermatas, the dialogue texture surrounding the return of the half-step motive, as well as the strong tonic cadence in F minor all suggest m. 238.[7]

It seems evident, then, that the draft encapsulates many defining elements of the final section. These include the general melodic plan, with material from the exposition recurring in the same order, *P, T, S*;

[7] A similar interaction between ideas for the development and for the coda occurs in the sketches for Op. 30 No. 2/I. A development draft on fo. 56[v]/st. 7 of the Kessler Sketchbook shows the secondary theme in the development in the key of the Neapolitan, D flat major. In the final version, Beethoven used A flat major for this spot and transferred the D flat major presentation of the theme to the coda. An explicit linking of development and coda sections also emerges from a study of sketches for the Pastoral Symphony. See Gossett, 'Beethoven's Sixth Symphony: Sketches for the First Movement', pp. 268–79.

Ex. 26. CD for the development, Part E

* rhythm unclear

the harmonic scaffolding, with three main key areas—E/e, A flat, and D flat—defined, and the latter functioning as the main point of arrival; and, lastly, the dynamic curve, in which the end of the development becomes a high point, with intensification sustained by a recall of the half-step motive from *P* linking into the recapitulation.

Subsequent to the continuity draft, we find two additional sketches for Part A. The first concerns mm. 68–75 (Ex. 27).[8] While the melodic profile at the beginning of this entry matches the final version, the ensuing passage focusing on the trills (mm. 71 ff.) is heavily revised. Two versions of the harmony for this segment appear. In the first, the dominant of E major resolves to its tonic before moving on to the supertonic; the supertonic (F♯) is then prolonged for the remainder of the sketch. In the second version the dominant moves directly to the supertonic, postponing tonic resolution for two measures, thereby increasing tension and continuity; an additional juxtaposition of tonic and supertonic chords activates the harmonic rhythm at the close. There is a melodic revision as well. Whereas the first version outlines a rising fifth at the moment of syncopation (f♯'–c♯²), the second version substitutes the interval of a fourth (e'–a'). This change,

[8] The darker ink and more vigorous writing style expressed on p. 193/sts. 14–15 suggest that these sketches for *S* are later than the sketches in paler ink on the upper staves.

Ex. 27. Sketch for Part A

doubtlessly motivated by the altered harmonic progression, has the added advantage of bolstering the relationship between this segment and *S*, because in both instances the interval of a fourth is associated with syncopation (Ex. 28). A final sketch for this area drafts the melody of mm. 76–7 (Ex. 29).

Ex. 28. Syncopation in first movement, mm. 37 and 74 compared

Ex. 29. Sketch for the development, Part A

The six additional sketches for Part B progress on several fronts (Ex. 30). In them we see Beethoven trying out specific harmonies, particularly for the end of the section; experimenting with strategies for organizing the phrase structure; and exploring ways of shaping the melody and the texture. To facilitate the discussion of these sketches I have arranged them in a suggested chronological order, listing their phrase structure, total length, and harmonic implications (Table 10). From a comparison of this data we can make the following observations about Part B at this compositional phase.

Ex. 30. Sketches for the development, Part B

1. *Length*

Only sketches 1 and 5 outline all of the section, and both of these are longer than the final version. Sketch 1 is more expansive at both the beginning and the end of the section, while sketch 5 is longer only at the end.

2. *Harmony*

Although Beethoven seems to have established the basic harmony of mm. 79–86 very quickly (a descent in major thirds from E minor to A flat major already appears in sketch 1), he was less sure of how to accomplish the pivot into D flat major (mm. 89–92 in the final version). A review of the alternatives found for this passage as compared with the final version follows.

TABLE 10. *Phrase structure and harmony, first movement, development, Part B: Final version (mm. 79–92) and six sketches compared*

		Measures						
		79–80	81–2	83–4	85–6	88–8	89–90	91–2
Final version (14mm.)	Phrase length:	⎡2	+ 2⎤ 4	⎡2	+ 2⎤ 4	⎡2	+ 2⎤ 4	⎡3 × ½ + 2 × ¼⎤ 2
	Harmony:	e: i / c: ♮iii	V_7	Ab: i / iii	V_2	Db: I / V	V_2^0	V_7–V_2^0
Sketch 1 (p.196/sts.1–5; 17mm.)	Phrase length:	2	4	2	2	2	2	2 + 1
	Harmony:	e: i / c: ♮iii	V_7	Ab: i / iii	V_2	iv_4^6	V_9^0	I–iv I / Db:V
Sketch 2 (p.190/st.13a; 2mm.)	Phrase length:	—	—	—	—	—	—	2
	Harmony:							Ab: I–V_9^0

Sketch 3
(p. 190/st. 13b;
6mm.)

Phrase length:	—	2	2	½	(incomplete)
Harmony:	c: i				
	Ab: iii	V_3^4	V	bvi degree	
		Db: I			

Sketch 4
(p. 193/sts. 6–7;
5mm.)

Phrase length:	—	—	—	1 1 1 1½ ½
Harmony:			Db:	$V–A_6–V–A_6–V$

Sketch 5
(p. 196/sts. 6–9;
15¼mm.)

Phrase length:	2	2	2	2	2	3+
Harmony:	c: i	V_7				
	c: ♮iii		Ab: iii			
				V_2^4	I	V_9^0
			Ab: iii		Db: I	$V–A_6$

Sketch 6
(p. 196/sts. 11–12;
9mm.)

Phrase length:	—	—	3 1	2	1½
Harmony:			Ab: $V–V_7$	$V–V_9^0/V–$	V_9^0	V
				Db:	

Note:
Dashes indicate absence of material; wavy lines indicate oscillating harmonics on a stationary bass or upper voices.

Sketch 1 delays the arrival of A flat major as a temporary tonic by resolving the dominant seventh of A flat to the minor subdominant (D flat minor). An exchange between the tonic and the minor subdominant in A flat follows; in retrospect, this might be intended as a minor-mode anticipation of the upcoming point of arrival on D flat major. However, the minor form of this chord never appears again.

Sketch 2 offers a more conventional choice for highlighting the articulation point: a dominant pedal on A♭ supports oscillating chords on A♭ and its diminished seventh. Sketch 3, which presents only the bass, implies a return to the idea of an upper neighbour-tone embellishment for the A♭ (B♭♭, in the last measure), a solution tried earlier in the continuity draft for the development (See Ex. 21, version 1). In sketch 4, if we accept my interpretation of B♭ as B♭♭, half-step motion in the bass is expanded and made integrative, because the regular alternation between A♭ and B♭♭ (or the fifth to the flat sixth degree in D flat major) now functions as a transposed melodic inversion of the original half-step motive on D♭–C. Beethoven retained this idea for the final version, where the B♭♭ is spelt as A♮ (a spelling already present in sketch 6).

Sketch 5 shows that the B♭♭ was to be harmonized by an augmented-sixth chord (B♭♭ in the bass, G♮ in the soprano, resolving in both voices to A♭). Near the end of sketch 6, however, Beethoven substituted a diminished-seventh chord. We may speculate that he retained this latter chord in the final version for two reasons: first, the G♭ contained by implication in the diminished-seventh chord has a stronger pull towards D flat major than the G♮ in the augmented-sixth chord; and, secondly, the diminished-seventh chord is a more consistent choice because its sound saturates the movement, particularly at articulation points in conjunction with the dominant. Beethoven did not discard the powerful effect of the augmented-sixth chord, however, but saved it for the theme of the second movement, where in m. 6 the chord appears in the same key to create fresh colour and add tension in an otherwise diatonic and unusually static melody.

3. *Phrase structure*
The basically duple structure of the final version is expressed in all of the entries, with one exception. This is sketch 6, which begins at a midpoint, on the dominant of A flat major. The phrase organization here suggests a broadening-out to three-measure units, followed by a contraction. This effect—one of increased excitement, generated by increasingly shorter phrases to close the section—was ultimately retained for the final version, where there is a carefully graduated pattern of quickening phrase rhythm (mm. 89–92).

4. *Melodic shape*

In the final version of Part B, repeated notes replace the downward octave leap of the original *Pax* motive. The sketches show this variant emerged as the result of trial and error. In sketch 1, for example, Beethoven eliminated the leap and replaced it with an extra occurrence of the trochaic rhythm. He must have rejected this idea as being too monotonous, because in sketches 3 and 5 he went back to the original motive. The final version emerges quite suddenly in sketch 6, although it may have been taken from an earlier coda sketch on p. 187/sts. 11–12. Beethoven's solution here maintains its connection with the original motive, yet adds a subtle touch of novelty.

5. *Texture*

The dialogue texture of the final version appears in sketch 5. The layout in its final bars mirrors the massive sound Beethoven sought in order to intensify the end of Part B (mm. 91–2), as both hands spread outwards to incorporate a vast musical space.

There are no additional sketches for Part C of the development, but the two entries for Part D focus on the secondary theme. The first sketch (Ex. 31*a*) offers an alternative for the end of the second phrase that was ultimately rejected: the harmony moves directly from D flat major to the dominant of F minor, skipping over the intervening harmony of B flat minor; also noteworthy is the hint of the half-step motive in the melodic profile of the accompaniment (see the oscillation between F and E♮).

The last sketch (Ex. 31*b*) refines the opening phrase of S, adding a dynamic marking (*pp*, analogous to the *p* in m. 109) and a reshaping of the cadence, so that the melodic line rises rather than falls. This last revision clears the way for potential growth, and thus predicts a

Ex. 31. Sketches for the development, Part D

crucial aspect of the movement—the transformation of S—an aspect that, unfortunately, is not documented in any of these sketches.

An unmeasured sketch on p. 197/st. 12 (Ex. 32) implies the alternation of hands and patterning found in Part E of the final version: the undifferentiated sixteenth-note rhythm of the sketch will appear in mm. 125–9 of the retransition.

Ex. 32. Sketch for the development, Part E

p.197/st.12

Finally, we come to the sketches on p. 203, the last page in Mendelssohn 15 to be concerned with Op. 57. This page, which is entirely devoted to the development section, presents several problems. First, it is preceded by both the stub of a missing leaf (designated in Tyson's inventory of Mendelssohn 15 as leaf E) and an interpolated bifolium with sketches for the Triple Concerto, Op. 56 (pp. 199–202 in the manuscript). As a result, there is a gap in continuity between p. 198 and p. 203. Furthermore, the sketches themselves seem to reflect at least two different compositional phases: while ideas at the top (st. 1) and bottom (sts. 12–15) have clear analogues in the final version, those in the middle of the page seem more remote, suggesting an earlier genesis. Also perplexing are the several indications for continuation (for example, the crosses appearing at the end of st. 1 and st. 11, and the middle of st. 9; and the '= de' at the beginning of st. 11), because the sequence of events they are intended to specify is not always evident. Keeping these reservations in mind, I shall nevertheless attempt to summarize the occurrences on this page (see Part V, the transcription of p. 203).

St. 1 seems to form a continuation of a sketch begun elsewhere, perhaps on the missing leaf; its patterning suggests the right hand in mm. 91–2, the end of Part B in the final version. After an empty space (presumably intended to allow for the hypothetical insertion of the transition theme in D flat, i.e. Part C), the melodic line picks up with the lead-in to the secondary theme in D flat major (mm. 100–5 in the final version). A cross in the right-hand corner then points to st. 9b, where this chromatic line is repeated in augmentation, and extended to Gb (on st. 10); the theme itself never appears.

St. 2 is empty, but the cancelled measures on sts. 3/4 suggest a relationship with the counter-statement of the primary theme in the exposition (PT, mm. 17–23). The thick chordal texture, and the

syncopation implied here, suggest Beethoven might have been thinking of recalling some aspect of this function for use in the development.

Sts. 6–11 seem to present a draft of Part B, although any conclusion
we might make about this section must be qualified by noting the
problems faced in making a transcription here. First of all, we are
hampered by the inconsistency of the clef changes; secondly, even
when we manage to establish a grammatically coherent reading, the
key plan (in C minor, a stepwise ascent from G to C, followed by a
series of thirds falling to D flat) seems strangely regressive when
compared to drafts for Part B found earlier in the sketchbook (on
p. 196). In fact, the opening on the dominant of C minor outlined on
st. 6/mm. 2–3 is a throwback to preliminary attempts for the development, in which C minor was implied as the tonal goal (see, for
example, the end of CD II for the exposition, Ex. 19e).[9]

The fabric of these mid-page staves also recollects elements seen in
previous sketches for Part E, the retransition section. The stepwise
ascent from G to C, for example (sts. 6–7), recalls the rising bass found
in the continuity draft for the development (p. 194/st. 12), while the
patterning for the right hand at the end of st. 11 is similar to the close of
that same draft (p. 194/sts. 13–14), as well as to several fragments
found on p. 195 (see sts. 6 and 8) and p. 193 (st. 4b).[10]

Sketches towards the bottom of p. 203 (sts. 12/13 and 14/15)
concentrate on details for the end of the retransition (mm. 129–35). In
the first version of this passage only the percussive rhythm of the half-
step motive returns; in the second, Beethoven included the melody as
well. Although the same melodic motive is recalled at the end of the
continuity draft (p. 194/st. 14), this sketch on p. 203 seems later,
because Beethoven has replaced the tonic resolution of the motive
found there with the dominant pedal-point bridging this articulation
in the final version.

In conclusion, p. 203 may be the continuation of a continuity draft
begun on a page now lost to us. But it is also possible that all or part
of the page functioned as a kind of collective centre for working
out problematic passages in the development. This latter suggestion would explain why so many of the sketches focus on refining

[9] Although it may appear inconsistent for Beethoven to return to preliminary ideas
at a late stage, he does so elsewhere. For an example in sketches for the development of
the finale of the Second Symphony, see Bathia Churgin, review of *Ludwig van
Beethoven: Kesslersches Skizzenbuch*, ed. Sieghard Brandenburg (Bonn, 1976–8), *Israel
Studies in Musicology*, 3 (1983), 177.

[10] It is difficult to know whether the fragments on pp. 195 and 193 were intended
for the end of the development or for the climax in the coda, since they occur in
isolation; in both cases the figuration is similar.

connective tissue rather than on main events, and would also account for the different phases of composition they apparently reflect.

As might be expected, only a few sketches appear for the recapitulation. The opening bars of the primary theme occur on p. 196/st. 15a, prefaced by the connective sign '= de', but the matching part to this sign is not found (Ex. 33). The remaining entries concentrate on the transition area.[11] In one, the harmonies constituting mm. 160–3 of the final version appear; there is some repetition, making the passage longer and showing a variant of the left hand Beethoven ultimately rejected, in which the thirds descend (Ex. 34a). In another sketch (Ex. 34b) Beethoven experimented with a contrast in sound to high-light the border between the end of the primary-theme area and the beginning of the transition: the analogue to mm. 162–3 is in the lower register, while the transition begins in the higher register, so that the demarcation between the two is emphasized. For the final version Beethoven compressed the length and retained the higher register for the whole passage; this allowed him to elide the articulation, yielding a smoother effect and intensifying continuity.

Ex. 33. Recapitulation sketch for *P*

Ex. 34. Recapitulation sketches for *T*

(a)

[11]   Donald Greenfield has pointed out that recapitulation sketches for Op. 18 No. 1/I also centre on the transition. See his 'Sketch Studies for Three Movements of Beethoven's String Quartets, Op. 18 Nos. 1 and 2', Ph.D. dissertation (Princeton University, 1983), fos. 177–81.

Finally, a late addition on p. 192 in the sketchbook hints at the syncopated rhythm and decorative appoggiaturas that animate the second phrase of *T* in both the recapitulation and the exposition of the final movement (Ex. 34*c*). This fragment may also be the source for the variant of *T* enunciated in mm. 97–9 of the development.[12]

---

[12] Another case in which the final version of an event in the exposition is found only in sketches for the recapitulation occurs in the sketches for Op. 30 No. 2/I. A draft for the development, recapitulation, and coda (Kessler Sketchbook, fo. 59ᵛ) adumbrates the final version of the third phrase of the primary theme as it will appear in mm. 13–22 of the exposition.

7.   First Movement: Coda

There are four continuity drafts for the coda—more than for any previous section of the movement. Despite the strong possibility that not all the sketches for Op. 57 have survived, the disproportionately large amount of material extant for this section suggests its importance for Beethoven. Even more striking is that a considerable number of ideas were either suppressed or substantially altered for the final version. Some of the rejected ideas resemble material found in the final version of the coda of the third movement, thereby substantiating the close relationship between these two movements explored in our discussion of the final version.

Preliminary sketches for the coda appear at an early stage of work on the movement, immediately following CD I for the exposition (Ex. 35).[1] Already established in Beethoven's initial attempt is the texture framing the final version of this section: a tremolo in the right hand, combined with a motive from P in the left hand. The variant of P used here, with repeated notes replacing the original octave leap, actually closes the final coda (m. 260), and is also used in Part B of the development (mm. 79–90). Two other elements in this sketch that shape the final terminus are the fermata and the low F in the left hand.

Ex. 35. Early coda sketch

Additional sketches appear on the neighbouring page of the manuscript. In one (Ex. 36a) Beethoven stabilized F minor by an alternation of tonic and dominant harmonies, culminating in a rising arpeggio on the tonic. Integration with previous material is achieved by using the

---

[1] Similarly, in sketches for Op. 30 No. 2/I an idea for the end of the coda precedes entries for the development. See the Kessler Sketchbook, fo. 55ᵛ/st. 1.

Ex. 36. Early coda sketches

trills from *Pay* in the bass. In a second sketch Beethoven combined a scalar figure with *Pax* in the bass; here, the harmony sits firmly on the dominant (Ex. 36b).

Two other early ideas appear on p. 193. The first presents descending figuration in A flat minor; similar figuration surfaces in later coda sketches, but in the tonic key (Ex. 37a). The second idea is for the beginning of the coda; it consists of two complementary parts, both of which employ the distinctive trochaic rhythm of *P* (Ex. 37b). The opening phrase rises, while the response begins in the treble and descends, melodizing a diminished-seventh chord and terminating on the dominant of F minor. Both phrases of this sketch will reappear in CD II.

On p. 192 we find the first continuity draft (Ex. 38). It is approximately twenty measures long and draws on many of the preliminary

Ex. 37. Additional early coda sketches

ideas explored above.[2] For purposes of discussion, we can make the following subdivisions.

Part A

The opening segment of five measures, like Beethoven's initial sketch on p. 187/sts. 11–12, displays the tremolo texture framing the final coda, but a progressive feature is the higher register of the tremolo. A pause on a diminished chord (with fermata) punctuates the close of this segment.

Part B

Next we find an aborted notation for an imitative idea that has already appeared on several previous pages of the manuscript. Beethoven tried repeatedly to knit this motive into the fabric of the coda; its significance will be treated separately at the end of this chapter.

Part C

The third segment, marked 'fine', returns to *Pax* material in the bass with a throbbing chordal accompaniment in the right hand. Harmonic activity consists of a supporting tonic pedal beneath a cadential progression in F minor, i–bII–V–i. The tonic–Neapolitan relationship, with the bII appearing in root position, makes explicit reference to the opening gesture of the sonata. Also noteworthy is the double bar at the end of sts. 15/16, which implies that the fortissimo chord placed there was originally intended to close the movement. Beethoven later crossed out the penultimate measure of this section (and probably meant to delete the final one as well), adding six new measures above the draft, on st. 13b.

Part D

The appended measures fuse the trochaic rhythm of *Pax* with the following material from the preliminary sketch on p. 188/st. 6: the trills, the tonic–dominant alternation, the rising melodic contour peaking on a high f^3, and the concluding fermata.

As we can see, even at this early stage Beethoven envisaged a coda of substantial breadth. It would include several contrasting parts, introduce new material (the imitative idea), and also recall material from earlier parts of the movement.

Two small sketches on p. 194 intervene before the second draft. The first (Ex. 39a) displays several measures of tonic harmony, a broad

---

[2] The draft on p. 192 is later than preliminary sketches on p. 193, as is clear from the 'Vi . . . 2' indication on p. 193/st. 12, which points backwards to the matching referrent, '2', at the head of p. 192/st. 13.

Ex. 38. CD I for the coda

melodic curve, and the *Pax* motive (although not with its characteristic rhythm) in a closing position; these elements all appear in the final version, mm. 257–62. The sketch breaks off inconclusively, although Beethoven punctuates it with his usual symbol for a double bar. The second entry (Ex. 39*b*) foreshadows the triple subdivision of the beat characteristic of Part E in the final coda (mm. 249–56).[3]

The second continuity draft, which appears on p. 195 (Ex. 40), is slightly longer than the first. The following comparison points out the similarities as well as the rearrangements and substitutions of material found in CD II.

Part A

This segment is approximately the same length as its analogue in CD I. However, the inner proportions are altered to create more tension: the tremolo on the tonic is abbreviated (from four to three measures), while the ensuing dissonant harmony is expanded. The diminished

[3] It is also possible that this sketch was intended for the coda of the finale; the harmonic rhythm is similar to that in III/mm. 340–52. In any case, this ambiguity adds another connective thread between these two movements.

Ex. 39. Coda sketches

seventh of the dominant is also recast as a metrically free, rising arpeggio leading to a diminished seventh of the tonic. Different shades of ink on st. 12 alert us to Beethoven's later embellishment of the dramatic cadence on db², producing a new extension of the half-step motive, to Db–C–Bb, which implies impending resolution.

Part B
Initially, it seems that Beethoven intended to substitute the first phrase from a preliminary sketch (on p. 193/st. 8) for the imitative motive found at this juncture; but a second layer in darker ink (st. 12) reverts to the pattern established for Part B in CD I. The 'presto' indication belongs to the first layer, suggesting that closing with a climactic tempo acceleration was an early idea. Later, Beethoven would transfer the rubric 'presto' to the coda of the finale, and substitute the tempo contrasts 'Adagio: più allegro' for this point in the coda.

Part C
Like its analogue in CD I, this segment is based on *P*; here, however, Beethoven inverts the material so that the motive sounds in the right hand, with a chordal accompaniment over a tonic pedal in the left hand. The F–Gb juxtaposition in the melody now becomes a point of departure for a linear ascent, extending through Gb to Ab. The second phrase from the preliminary sketch on p. 193/st. 8 is newly added to make a smoother connection into Part D.

Part D
The final segment (a later addition) replaces the trills found in CD I with a return of the tremolo texture and closes on a rising arpeggio in F minor (perhaps taken from the preliminary sketch on p. 188/st. 6). Beethoven intensified the ending of his previous draft by stretching

Ex. 40. CD II for the coda

the melodic peak an additional actave to f³, reinforcing the fortissimo with crescendo and pedal indications, and exaggerating the trochaic rhythm in the penultimate measure (from ♩. ♪ to ♩.. ♪).

After CD II, tentative growth continues in four small sketches. On p. 196/st. 15b (Ex. 41) two ideas plucked from earlier pages are recombined: the trills from the sketch on p. 188/st. 6; and the arpeggiated descent on a diminished-seventh chord from CD II. The trills, now in the soprano, embellish repeated motion from F to G. The harmony implied here (alternating tonic and dominant chords, followed by motion to the subdominant) may have some bearing on mm. 243–4 in the final coda, while the subsequent diminished-seventh chord probably relates to the cadenza-like section (mm. 218–38 in the final version).

Ex. 41. Coda sketches

On p. 197/st. 1 we find another sketch incorporating a triple subdivision of the beat (Ex. 42), but with a new emphasis on repeated notes that anticipates Part E of the final coda. The peak note (f³), the dotted rhythm, and the fermata are all gleaned from the conclusion of CD II, and thus, even though there is no double bar, we can assume this sketch relates to the end of the coda. Two more fragments on the same page are harmonically important. The first of these predicts the motion from F minor to D flat major that will eventually be expanded at the beginning of the coda (Ex. 43a); the second points towards the tonic resolution of S (mm. 239–48), as the melodic outline and syncopated rhythm of this theme are briefly suggested here (Ex. 43b).

Ex. 42. Coda sketches

Ex. 43. Coda sketches

The third draft (p. 197/sts. 14–16; Ex. 44) follows an entry for the end of the recapitulation (mm. 201–3 in the final version). Part A begins with *Pax* material in the bass and closes with an augmentation of the half-step motive on Db–C, sustained by a fermata; unlike previous drafts, however, the harmony includes the F minor–D flat major progression sketched above the draft (Ex. 43*a* above).

Part B has no parallel in CD I or II, but relates to the sketches featuring triplet eighths. Beethoven adds ties here to inject rhythmic tension. A modified version of this rhythm, with rests replacing the ties, characterizes Part E of the final coda. Further kinship with the final version is apparent in the melodic emphasis on the three-note motive C–Db–C at the end of this segment, and on the harmonic tendency towards the subdominant chord of B flat minor at the beginning of st. 15.[4]

Part C returns to *Pax* material; a rising bass moves by step from dominant to tonic in F minor, then breaks off inconclusively on a repeated G, possibly implying a dominant (or supertonic?) chord. No clue indicates how Beethoven intended to finish this sketch, which is clearly incomplete.

Finally we come to the fourth draft (p. 198/sts. 4–8; Ex. 45). It is the most compressed but, as in previous instances, falls naturally into four sections. Part A uses *Pax* material in conjunction with the i–bII progression in F minor. Part B continues the same trochaic rhythm-pattern to reaffirm the tonic (perhaps anticipating the tonic resolution of the secondary theme in mm. 240–8 of the final version?). Part C, in triplet rhythm, incorporates the emphasis on the half-step motive seen in Part B of CD III, together with a new cadential pattern, harmonized in the final version as: i–V/V–i$^6_4$–V (mm. 251 and 254–6). Part D presents an expansive transformation of the arpeggiated flourish concluding CD II: several measures of brilliant passagework extend the upper border to C^4, while an oscillating motion between tonic and dominant harmonies generates stability. All of this figuration eventually

---

[4] B flat minor lends a tragic cast to the thematic transformation of *S*, mm. 243–4 and 246–7 in the final version.

Ex. 44.   CD III for the coda

Ex. 45.   CD IV for the coda

* barline omitted as unnecessary

became part of the main climax (mm. 218–38). Although no tempo change is marked here, the gradual rhythmic progression—from eighths, to triplet eighths, to sixteenths—acts as a written-out accelerando, suggesting a connection with the 'presto' written in the first layer of CD II, Part B.

Table 11 compares the structure of these continuity drafts with the final version. While I have treated CD IV as a separate entity, it is also possible that it was intended as an appendix to CD III, because, when we merge the two drafts, the layout approximates the sixfold design of the final version. In this case, Part A of CD IV would constitute an extension of Part C in CD III; Part B would be the forerunner of Part D in the final coda; Part C would be the analogue of Part E; and Part D would correspond to the final closing section, Part F. The problem with this interpretation is that the coda would then contain *two* distinct sections in triplet eighths; however, given the modest role envisaged at this stage for the secondary theme, it could be that Beethoven was thinking of giving this rhythmic intensification more exposure than he did in the final coda.

There is some evidence in the autograph that the ending outlined in CD IV represents a rather advanced phase in Beethoven's view of the conclusion. On the last system of p. 19 the first measure is crossed out and beneath the ink scratches we find a notation for the right hand, resembling the rising arpeggio near the end of CD IV. This suggests that the more subdued close of the final version was the result of a late decision (Fig. 3, p. 106).

Several additional coda studies are worth mentioning. Below CD IV is a sketch marked with the connective '= de' (Ex. 46). The nearest companion referent, 'Vi:', appears on the previous page, at the close of

Ex. 46. Coda sketch

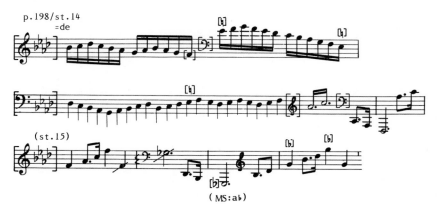

TABLE 11. Coda, first movement: Final version (mm. 204–62) and continuity drafts compared

	Final version	CD I (p.192/sts.13–16)	CD II (p.195/sts.10–15; sts.1/2)	CD III (p.197/sts.14–16)	CD IV (p.198/sts.4–8)
Length	59mm.	c.20mm.	c.23mm. (?)	19mm. (incomplete)	16mm.
Growth	6 parts★	4 parts	4 parts	3 parts	4 parts
	A tremolo/*Pax*; F–Gb gesture	A tremolo/*Pax*; seed of cadenza; fermata	A tremolo/*Pax*; seed of cadenza; *Pb* motive; fermata.	A tremolo/*Pax*; *Pb* motive; fermata	A *Pax*, F–Gb gesture
	B *S* in Db	B imitative motive	B imitative motive replaces rising bass	B triplet theme (seed of *NK*)	B *Pax* variant, all on tonic (seed of *S*?)
	C cadenza; *Pb* motive; fermata	C F–Gb gesture; tonic pedal	C F–Gb gesture; treble answer	C *Pax* ascending, from V–i; breaks off inconclusively	C triplet theme; ends with *Pb* motive
	D *S* in tonic	D trill idea; last note with fermata	D tremolo/*Pax*; rising flourish on tonic		D brilliant cadenza-like ending; singing-song effect on V–I harmonies
	E *NK*—Triplet theme.				
	F tremolo/*Pax*				
Sound	*ppp* ending	*ff* ending	*ff* ending intensified by crescendo and pedal		
Melody	Upper peak: c⁴	Upper peak: f²	Upper peak: f³	Upper peak: f³	Upper peak: c⁴
Rhythm	Tempo acceleration after Part C (m.238: Adagio; più Allegro). Part E features triplet eighths and syncopation, highlighted by *sf* accents	No tempo change	Tempo change to presto (version 1)	Triplet eighths with ties inject rhythmic tension	Triplet eighths with ties as in CD III
		No triplet eighths. Dotted rhythm in final bar	No triplet eighths. Dotted rhythm of final bar is intensified		Systematic acceleration in surface rhythm relates to presto in CD II and più Allegro
Harmony†	f–Db–f(bb)–f	all in f	all in f	f–(Db)–f–(bb)–f	all in f NB p.198/sts.14–15: perhaps a revision of CD IV

★ For the division of the final version into Parts A–F, see Ch. 1.

an elliptical entry for the imitative motive, on p. 197/st. 11b. The beginning of the sketch—brilliant passagework around the dominant of F minor—flows naturally from the close of this elliptical entry, and also suggests a kinship with the figuration marking the conclusion of CD IV. The remainder of the sketch, however, is confusing because it presents material associated, not with the end, but with the beginning (Part A) of CD IV: the tremolo texture with *Pax* in the bass, and an incomplete statement of the familiar i–bII gesture. Moreover, there are two deleted pitches, F–Gb (p. 198/st. 15), that appear to have been copied directly from the draft above. It is possible, therefore, that this sketch presents two different, non-adjacent sections of the coda. Perhaps Beethoven was revising certain aspects of the draft, not necessarily in order of their appearance.

A late sketch for Part E of the coda occurs as an addition to p. 190 (Ex. 47). The opening replicates the triplet rhythm found in CD IV, Part C, but two new features suggest it post-dates the draft: the metre is in 12/8 rather than 4/4; and an added accompaniment in the left hand fills out the cadence in more detail, anticipating mm. 251 and 254–6 of the final coda. The final three measures predict the general shape of mm. 257–62, because the melodic peak (f^3) and the final right-hand pitch (c^2) are both present here.

Ex. 47. Coda sketch

On the same page there is a monolinear harmonic plan that also may relate to the coda. Unfortunately, the progression it implies does not seem to refer to any specific passage in the final movement (Ex. 48).[5]

Several sketches focus on patterning for the diminished-seventh chord, E♮–G–Bb–Db, a sonority Beethoven clearly intended for the close of the cadenza-like section (Ex. 49a–d). Here we see him working on range (especially the high register for the melodic climax in m. 233 of the final section, although the harmony for this measure will be changed to a dominant-seventh chord); and on the recall of the

---

[5] The problem with understanding this harmonic progression concerns the second chord, which seems to imply the interval of an augmented sixth over Ab; however, this chord does not connect to a chord on Gb.

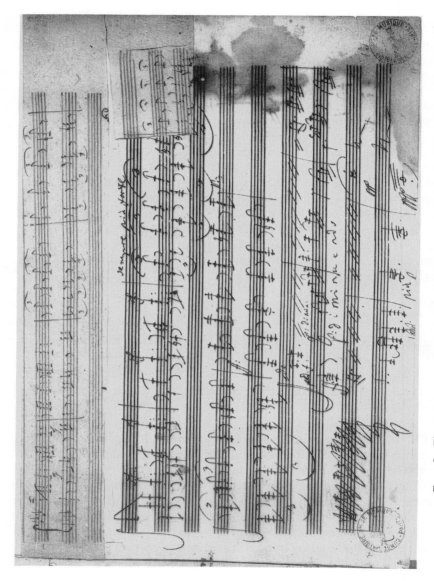

FIG. 3. First movement autograph (Bibliothèque Nationale, MS 20), p. 19

Ex. 48. Bassline sketch

half-step motive (Ex. 49*e*). Finally, there is a fragment reminiscent of
PT (Ex. 49*f*). Its presence on a page devoted exclusively to coda ideas
suggests Beethoven may have been considering it for a closing gesture.
The half-step motion (C–D♭) in the final measure, as well as the
alternation of hands at the end of the sketch, anticipate the hemiola
effect he ultimately adopted for mm. 251 and 254–6 of the final
section.

Ex. 49. Sketches for coda, diminished-seventh chord

In summary, we can see that the early sketches and continuity drafts reveal Beethoven's determination to include certain motives and textures in the coda. The purposeful reiteration of the Neapolitan relationship; the framing tremolo texture; the tempo acceleration; the climactic cadenza punctuated by a dramatic pause on a diminished-seventh chord with fermata; the inclusion of a unit based on *P*, that rises by step—these are key elements that appear early and survive the entire process. On the other hand, the sketches also demonstrate the rich collateral flow nourishing Beethoven's compositional efforts; we see him weeding out many ideas that were either inappropriate or redundant. The trills from *Pay*, for example, found twice in these sketches, were probably discarded because they constitute the principal melodic material for Part A in the development. The imitative motive present in CD I and II was also ultimately suppressed, and the reasons for this will be discussed below.

Several early ideas that were retained appear in expanded form, or are completely transformed. Chief among the former is the laconic diminished-seventh chord with fermata, which grows into a section of twenty measures. The latter category includes the pointed allusion to the Neapolitan relationship (F–G♭), which Beethoven would develop into the opening event of the coda, reharmonizing the G♭ as part of a dominant seventh of D flat major (mm. 205–6). Structurally, this was an economical revision, because the G♭ could work to recall the characteristic half-step gesture of the movement and simultaneously reintroduce D flat major, the main point of harmonic arrival in the development.

In many respects CD III and IV, together with their satellite sketches, bring the final coda into view. The expansion of the tonal plan to include motion towards D flat major and B flat minor, the incorporation of a section featuring a triplet-eighth rhythm and a melody based on *P*, the extension of the upper border from f^3 to c^4, all hint at events found in the completed work.

One of the more unexpected discoveries is that Beethoven originally planned to conclude the first movement with an emotional climate that might be called heroic or defiant.[6] This *Affekt* is suggested by the fortissimo markings ending CD I and II, and in the expansive melodic ascent terminating CD II and IV. Beethoven chose to recast this ending, and we can surmise he did so for several reasons. First, he had to consider the architecture of the movement as a whole: by ending the movement *ppp* and keeping the right-hand figuration in the middle

[6] For a discussion of other works during this period that generate a similarly triumphant feeling at the close, see Alan Tyson, 'Beethoven's Heroic Phase', *Musical Times*, 110 (1969), 139–41.

register, he would allow the coda to share the same melodic and dynamic curve delineating earlier sections. Since the exposition, development, recapitulation, and coda all begin and end in the low register in the left or both hands, this change worked to further unity and symmetry. Furthermore, it had the advantage of providing a more natural link into the soft dynamic and low register beginning the second movement.

It is also probable that, after working on the subsequent movements, Beethoven realized that the triumphant expression of this 'heroic' ending could serve more effectively as a goal for the whole sonata. Elements from these sketches that resurface in a new guise in the final version of the third movement include the *cresc.–ff* ending from CD II (mm. 334–53), the 'presto' from CD II (m. 308), the harmonic progression, i–bII–V–i, from CD I (mm. 326–33), and the brilliant, sixteenth-note passage over tonic and dominant harmonies from CD IV (mm. 341–53). Thus, these sketches underscore the remarkable flexibility of many of Beethoven's ideas; rejected for use in one context, they often found a place in another more appropriate environment.[7]

THE IMITATIVE MOTIVE

The little imitative motive which comprises Part B in both CD I and II for the coda is curious because, unlike most of the other material in these sketches, it has no parallel in the final version. Furthermore, it is not unique to these drafts, appearing no fewer than eight times, beginning with the preliminary exposition sketches on p. 187, and continuing intermittently until p. 197 (sketches 1–8 are given in Ex. 50). At most, the motive lasts for three measures; in one case, it consists of just three notes plus an 'etc'. The motive always begins in F minor with the same three pitches, and, although the succeeding pitches vary in each sketch, the melody consistently projects a similar melodic profile (a sharp rise followed by a descent).

How can we relate this motive to the thematic complex defining the first movement? The key and the opening pitches are not problematic: F minor is the tonic key, and the initial half-step relates to the *Pb* motive. The correspondence is particularly obvious in sketch 2, where the order of the opening pitches, Db–C, is the same. What is perplexing, however, is the metre. Although Beethoven experimented

---

[7] See Alan Tyson, 'The Problem of Beethoven's "First" Leonore Overture', *Journal of the American Musicological Society*, 28 (1975), 329, where Tyson shows how unused C-minor ideas for Op. 138 and Op. 59 No. 3 may have influenced the composition of Op. 62.

Ex. 50. Eight sketches for the imitative motive

with several different rhythmic designs, the melody is almost always in duple metre.[8] The one exception, sketch 2, shows a triple division of the beat, implying the 12/8 metre used for the final version. Although Beethoven used a mixed metrical notation for many of the first movement sketches, the strongly duple character of the motive suggests that, were it to be used, a change of metre might have been necessary.

[8] Beethoven subjected the primary theme of Op. 18 No. 1/I to similar rhythmic manipulation in the sketches. See *N II*, pp. 481–3. Although Nottebohm's remarks imply that all the sketches he transcribed there were intended for the beginning of the primary theme, more recent scholarship suggests some entries may have been intended for the close of the tonic area. See Greenfield, 'Sketch Studies for Three Movements of Beethoven's String Quartets, Op. 18 Nos. 1 and 2', fos. 48–61.

It is apparent from sketches 1 and 6 that Beethoven intended to treat the motive contrapuntally. In his discussion of the Op. 57 sketches, Nottebohm selected these two entries for transcription, calling the melody 'einem Nachahmungsmotiv' (hence the name, 'imitative motive').[9] In fact, the motive closely resembles a typical fugue subject, with long notes for the head and shorter ones for the tail; in sketches 2, 4, and 7 the tail is completely or partially sequential. Similar minor-key subjects occur in fugues of the Baroque and Classical periods.[10]

In his brief remarks Nottebohm recognized that the motive was intended for use in the 'zweiten Theil', although he was careful not to specify in which portion of the second part of the movement it was to appear. Normally in a sonata-form movement, the expected environment for a contrapuntal episode would be in the development. Two examples from Beethoven's middle period—one prior to Op. 57 and one later—might be invoked as evidence for this placement. The first is the String Quintet, Op. 29 (autograph dated 1801); the fourth movement contains a complex development fugato written in two metres, 6/8 and 2/4.[11] Similarly, the String Quartet, Op. 59 No. 1 (completed 1806), presents a long fugato in the development section of the first movement (mm. 185–209).[12]

But in this instance there is no evidence Beethoven intended to use the imitative motive in the development of Op. 57/I. Sketch 1 occurs below an idea for the end of the movement, but, like sketches 2 and 3, it is an isolated fragment and therefore cannot be linked with any specific function. Sketch 4 is adjacent to CD III of the exposition, but the thicker strokes and darker ink marking its appearance suggest it is a later addition to the page, and may therefore bear no relationship to the neighbouring exposition draft.

[9] See *N II*, p. 440.

[10] Beethoven's motive is related to the 'pathotype' formula discussed in Warren Kirkendale, *Fugue and Fugato in Rococo and Classical Chamber Music*, trans. Margaret Bent and the author (2nd edn., Durham, 1979), 91–2. Kirkendale explains that, in this subject-type, the pitch order usually follows the plan $5 \nearrow 6 \searrow 7 \nearrow 1$ (or some variant of this basic pattern). Beethoven's motive begins with the scale degrees $5 \nearrow 6 \nearrow 4$, replacing the characteristic leap of a descending diminished seventh with an ascending major sixth. An early example of Beethoven's use of this subject-type in a contrapuntal passage occurs in the first movement of his Trio, Op. 1 No. 2 (1794–95). For valuable remarks on this passage, see Richard Kramer, 'Notes to Beethoven's Education', *Journal of the American Musicological Society*, 28 (1975), 89–91.

[11] A discussion of this quintet is found in Churgin, 'Beethoven's Sketches'.

[12] On the compositional problems posed by this fugato as reflected in Beethoven's autograph revisions, see Richard Kramer, '"Das Organische der Fuge": On the Autograph of Beethoven's String Quartet in F major, Op. 59, No. 1', in Christoph Wolff (ed.), *The String Quartets of Haydn, Mozart and Beethoven* (Cambridge, Mass., 1980), 223–65.

The context of sketches 5 and 6, however, clarifies the issue; both are drawn from continuity drafts for the coda, and in each case the motive is preceded by the diminished-seventh chord with fermata. Sketches 7 and 8 are again isolated entries. It is possible they relate to one another, since they are only a few staves apart: the 'etc.' closing sketch 8 may be a shorthand notation for the sixteenth-notes in the tail of sketch 7.

Sketch 8, which is the shortest, has several puzzling aspects. It is preceded by a six–four chord with fermata, the traditional signal for a cadenza (note that this indication is congruent with the placement of the motive within CD I and II), and is followed by the inscription 'point d'orgue' over a low dominant pitch, the usual signal for a pedal-point. While both of these signs point to the coda, the 'Vi:' concluding the sketch injects confusion, because it could lead to either of two matching indications: the '= de' found on the previous p. 196/st. 15, a sketch for the beginning of the recapitulation; or the '= de' found on p. 198/sts. 14–15, a sketch for the coda. If we select the first alternative, it could mean that Beethoven was thinking of inserting an imitative section in duple metre near the close of the retransition. This structural device has roots in the 'da capo sinfonia', a popular form in the later eighteenth century.[13] A precedent for this idea is found in an early draft for Op. 31 No. 2/I (the Kessler Sketchbook, fo. 90ᵛ), where a slow section, marked 'dolce', is interpolated at the end of the development.[14] Since Beethoven had discarded this idea for Op. 31 No. 2, perhaps he was reconsidering it for Op. 57.

The unequivocal function of sketches 5 and 6, however, argues for the alternative conclusion, that sketch 8 links up with the coda idea on p. 198. In this case the imitative motive would have functioned as the basis for a section following the fermata, and the 'point d'orgue' would specify a dominant underpinning for the virtuosic figuration at the head of the coda sketch (transcribed in Ex. 46).[15] Beethoven had tried such a plan in a sketch for the rondo finale of the Triple Concerto, on p. 142/sts. 6–7 of Mendelssohn 15. Here we find an implied subdominant chord, sustained by a fermata and followed by the words 'cadenza fugato' and 'point d'orgue', over a low dominant

[13] On this term, see Jan LaRue, 'Sinfonia, 2' in *The New Grove Dictionary of Music and Musicians*, ed. Stanley Sadie (London, 1980), xvii. 337.

[14] See Barry Cooper, 'The Origins of Beethoven's D Minor Sonata Op. 31 No. 2', *Music and Letters*, 62 (1981), 261–80. Cooper's transcription of the draft appears on pp. 263–4.

[15] Leonard Ratner has shown that in the eighteenth century a cadenza could be indicated by any of the following terms: cadenza, fermata, arbitrio, and point d'orgue. See his *Classic Music*, p. 305.

pitch. This idea was actually retained for the final version of Op. 56/ III, where, beginning in m. 406, there is an imitative solo section connecting the end of the 2/4 episode with a return to the primary theme. Perhaps Beethoven was considering a comparable peroration in the coda of Op. 57/I.[16]

Beethoven's persistent efforts to find the right place for this little motive suggest he was reluctant to part with it; then why did he discard it? From the sketches, it would seem he was disturbed by two issues. The first involved the local problems he encountered when he tried to develop the motive. From the beginning he seemed to have difficulty fixing the relationship between subject and answer. Sketch 1, for example, outlines the entire subject, plus the beginning of a subdominant answer. While such a tonal relationship is not unusual in Beethoven's contrapuntal writing, in this case the answer is irregular because the scale degrees 5–6–4 in the tonic subject are answered by scale degrees 7–1–6 in the subdominant.[17] The only other contrapuntal entry (sketch 6) presents just the head of the motive in stretto-like imitation at the seventh. Neither sketch offers a traditional tonal answer for the subject, and maybe this was because Beethoven realized that this solution would distort the intervallic succession of the subject, forcing it to lose all connection—however tenuous–with previous thematic events.[18]

A second issue concerned the larger question of how to integrate an imitative episode with the rest of the movement. As we have seen in these sketches, Beethoven had just begun to extract the dramatic possibilities latent in the secondary theme, and thus he had not yet developed a protracted relationship between P and S. Perhaps the impetus for evolving this relationship was triggered by the difficulties he encountered with manipulating the imitative motive; or perhaps

[16] Lewis Lockwood points out that, in the first movement of the Violoncello Sonata, Op. 5 No. 1 in F major (1796), Beethoven begins the coda with a long cadenza for both instruments that leads to the final presentation of the primary theme and its cadential closure. See his 'Beethoven's Early Works for Violoncello and Pianoforte: Innovation in Context', *Beethoven Newsletter*, 1 (1986), 19.

[17] See Kirkendale, *Fugue and Fugato*, p. 270. Kirkendale observes that Beethoven uses a subdominant answer in the following works: Op. 35, Op. 55/IV, Op. 120, and Op. 131. Similarly, in the contrapuntal passage in Op. 1 No. 2/I mentioned above, the 'pathotype' subject presented in the violin, on D↗Eb↘F♮↗G (mm. 167–70), is answered in the piano, on G↗Ab↘B↗C (mm. 171–4). Here, however, the subdominant entrance is part of an overall spiral of descending fifths.

[18] A traditional tonal answer would require the following notes: $f'–ab'–f^2$, so that the minor second of the subject would be answered by a minor third, and the third pitch would be an octave above the first pitch, rather than a seventh. Seeing the difficulty with a traditional answer, Beethoven may have planned a freer type of imitative section.

the creative process worked in reverse. At any rate, once Beethoven had determined that the interplay between these two themes would direct the shape of the movement, he must have felt that a fugal episode, with its evocation of the 'learned style', would be antithetical to the impassioned *Sturm und Drang* character of the movement, and would also disrupt the delicate threads of continuity supporting the central thematic drama.[19]

One residual effect of Beethoven's preoccupation with the motive, however, may be the flashes of contrapuntal texture in the finale. The subdominant bias of the motive may also have influenced harmonic choices here, as this key area (B flat minor) figures prominently in the development section (see III/mm. 118–49).

A final point of interest resides in the kinship between the imitative motive and the primary theme and fugue subject for Beethoven's late quartets, Op. 132/I and Op. 133.[20] All three themes begin with an ascending second, followed by a rising sixth or diminished seventh (in the case of the imitative motive, the sixth is major rather than minor). The primary theme of Op. 131/I could also be related; the central skip of a descending major third is an inversion of the rising sixth of the motive, while the half-steps flanking the central skip are present in both cases.[21] One might also include the opening of the late Piano Sonata, Op. 111/I, where the 'Allegro con brio' theme begins with the scale degrees 1↗3↘7↗6; in both cases the melodic contour and rhythmic patterning are similar (Ex. 51).

Since we know it was Beethoven's habit to preserve discarded ideas for future use, it is possible that this little collection of rejected sketches for Op. 57/I became a source of inspiration, years later, for the genesis of these late themes.[22] Such an event has many precedents in Beethoven's workshop. Perhaps the most famous example concerns the 'Allegro con brio' theme for Op. 111/I. This theme originated as an incipit for

---

[19] In his late piano sonatas Beethoven succeeded in finding ways of using fugal textures towards the end of the work as a means of resolving tension. See, for example, his Piano Sonatas, Op. 106 and Op. 110, both of which have fugues in the final movements.

[20] The similarity between the imitative motive and the cantus for the late quartets is mentioned by Denis Matthews in his remarks on the recording 'Beethoven, The Piano Sonatas', in *Beethoven's Sketchbooks* (Discourse Records, Tunbridge Wells, 1974), disc 7, side 1.

[21] See Kirkendale, *Fugue and Fugato*, p. 267, where he discusses the relationship between the opening of Op. 132/I, the fugue subject for Op. 133, the primary theme for Op. 131/I, and the 'pathotype' formula. Kirkendale states: 'Beethoven is returning here to the Baroque art of varying theme types, specifically the "pathotype".'

[22] For the importance with which Beethoven regarded his sketchbooks, see Lockwood, 'On Beethoven's Sketches and Autographs', pp. 42–3.

Ex. 51. The imitative motive and late-period themes

the second movement of the Violin Sonata, Op. 30 No. 1, located in the Kessler Sketchbook (1801–2); although passed over for this work, it was recalled twenty years later for the piano sonata.[23] While we cannot know for certain if this is also the case with the imitative motive and these late themes, the connection nevertheless is there, forcing us to recognize the potency this melodic idea held for Beethoven over a long span of time.

[23] The incipit, part of an overall movement plan for the violin sonata, is found on fo. 37ᵛ. Gustave Nottebohm was the first to discuss the relationship between this sketch and Op. 111/I, in *Ein Skizzenbuch von Beethoven* (Leipzig, 1865); trans. Jonathan Katz, in *Two Beethoven Sketchbooks* (London, 1979). Mention of the sketch occurs on pp. 19 and 41 of the English version.

8. Second and Third Movements

Beethoven's sketches for the second movement suggest a different approach from that adopted for the first movement. We cannot be wholly certain about his working procedures here, because we have only a few entries, and these clearly stem from an early compositional phase; however, it seems that one determining factor may have been his choice of variation form.[1] No sustained drafts appear in these initial forays. Instead, there are short notations, usually no more than two or three measures long, in which Beethoven tried to capture some central ideas for the movement. Characteristic textures and rhythmic patterns occur, and occasionally there are specific remarks, as, for example, the 'triol[en]' on p. 190/st. 2b, or the 'senza repetizion(e)' on p. 191/st. 6b. Frequently these fragments break off with the indication 'etc.' (as on p. 190/st. 5b, or p. 191/st. 4a).

Among these notations, the 'concept' sketch on p. 195 typifies Beethoven's working methods at this early stage. As mentioned above, its main purpose was to establish an outline for the movement as a whole, and fix the variation types. In this way it served as a kind of matrix for future expansion.[2] In some middle-period works, and in most later variation sets, Beethoven experimented with two or more plans before choosing between them.[3] In other instances he evolved the final succession of the variations gradually as he worked on the

[1] See Sieghard Brandenburg, 'Beethovens "Erste Entwürfe" zu Variationenzyklen', in Carl Dahlhaus et al. (eds.), Bericht über den internationalen musikwissenschaftlichen Kongress Bonn 1970 (Kassel, 1971), 108–11, for a discussion of Beethoven's sketching procedures in other early variation cycles. Valuable information is also found in Lewis Lockwood, 'Beethoven's Earliest Sketches for the Eroica Symphony', Musical Quarterly, 67 (1981), 457–78; and in Christopher Reynolds, 'Ends and Means in the Second Finale to Beethoven's Op. 30 No. 1', in Lewis Lockwood and Phyllis Benjamin (eds.), Beethoven Essays: Studies in Honor of Elliot Forbes (Cambridge, Mass.; 1984), 127–45.

[2] A broader sketch plan, noting ideas for all movements of a cycle and focusing on the sequence of movements, is called a 'movement plan' by Lewis Lockwood. He notes that, while this type of sketch is found in Beethoven's late years, it is most prevalent between 1800 and 1804. See Lockwood, 'Beethoven's Earliest Sketches for the Eroica Symphony', pp. 460–1.

[3] For the variations on 'Rule Britannia', WoO 79 (1803), Beethoven made two separate outline sketches; the final version uses parts of each. See Brandenburg, 'Beethovens "Erste Entwürfe" zu Variationenzyklen', p. 110.

movement.[4] In this case, however, the order posited for the cycle in the 'concept' sketch was adapted for the final version.

The entire theme never appears in any of these sketches: we only see the opening two notes and the close of the melody. While Beethoven may have worked it out already elsewhere, it is also possible he was developing the melody simultaneously with work on the individual variations. This latter situation sometimes occurred when he was, as in this instance, using an original rather than a borrowed theme.[5]

In spite of their laconic nature, these notations are informative about many aspects of the final version, such as: (1) the duple metre and D flat major key of the movement; (2) the general architectural plan of division variations, with the final section recalling the register and texture of the opening; (3) the neighbour-tone figure motivating the contour of the theme, an important unifying device knit into the thematic structure of all three movements; and (4) the idea of linking the end of the Andante with the beginning of the finale. Because of the difficulty in determining the chronology of these brief sketches, I shall discuss them according to their order of appearance in the manuscript.

Three separate entries occur on p. 190. The first presents ideas for three variations: Var. 1 is in sixteenths; Var. 2 is in triplets, as indicated by the inscription 'triol[en]'; and Var. 3 is in thirty-seconds, as implied by the three lines drawn underneath the variation number.[6] The disposition of the parts in the third variation anticipates the exchange of melody and accompaniment governing the form of this double variation in the final version (Ex. 52a).

The second entry, which is marked 'Cd' (presumably an abbreviation

[4] In the course of sketching Op. 35, for example, Beethoven tried out various sequences for the cycle. See Christopher Reynolds, 'Beethoven's Sketches for the Variations in E♭, Op. 35', in *Beethoven Studies*, iii, ed. Alan Tyson (London, 1982), 61–2. For a discussion of the evolution of the formal organization in late sets of variations, see William Kinderman, 'The Evolution and Structure of Beethoven's "Diabelli" Variations', *Journal of the American Musicological Society*, 35 (1982), 306–28, and Meredith, 'The Sources for Beethoven's Piano Sonata in E Major, Op. 109', i. 372–496.

[5] Brandenburg suggests that a similar process, in which sketches for variations appear even before the theme itself is fully developed, occurs in sketches for Op. 30 No. 1/III. See 'Beethovens "Erste Entwürfe" zu Variationenzyklen', p. 110. This view is confirmed by Reynolds, 'Ends and Means in the Second Finale to Beethoven's Op. 30 No. 1'. Reynolds concludes that in this movement the 'genesis of the theme was not a question of arduous work that had to be completed before commencing the variations. Instead, the refinements of the theme are products of the variations . . . What has been thought to be a derivative relationship now should be viewed as reciprocal' (p. 142).

[6] This interpretation of the underlined numeral was suggested to me by Sieghard Brandenburg.

for 'coda') is in thirty-seconds; it could be intended as an early attempt for the link into Var. 4 (mm. 79–80 in the final version; see Ex. 52*b*). A third entry (Ex. 52*c*) confirms that the theme will begin with the pitches a♭–b♭, as already implied in the previous sketch for Var. 3. It is in two parts. The first part experiments with an off-beat formulation of the theme, ultimately adopted for Var. 1; the texture is complicated by a suggestion of an inner voice in sixteenth notes, an idea that was later delegated to Var. 2. The second part presents a varied pattern for the thirty-second notes of Var. 3.

Ex. 52. Sketches for the second movement

A different rhythmic succession for the cycle emerges on p. 191. The entry for Var. 1 is again in sixteenths (Ex. 53*a*). Var. 2 is also written in sixteenths, although the placement and quarter-note rhythm of the upper melody suggests that thirty-seconds were probably intended here (Ex. 53*b*). The entry for Var. 3 is in *triolen*; it seems there were to be two groups of triplet sixteenths to each beat. It is possible, therefore, that Beethoven was considering a reversal of the rhythmic progression from *triolen* to thirty-seconds outlined in the sketches on p. 190. At a later stage he would eliminate the *triolen* completely, and break up the quarter-notes of the theme more systematically, moving to eighths for Var. 1, and sixteenths for Var. 2, retaining the thirty-seconds for Var. 3.

Two additional structural aspects are apparent in the sketch complex on p. 191. First, the 'senza repetizione' at the end of st. 6 demonstrates that compressing the last variation by eliminating the repeats for each half of the theme was an early idea. In addition, the notation on st. 4b presents a statement of the link into the finale that is quite close to the final version (Ex. 53c). Significantly, no distinction is made between the two movements; they are neither independently labelled, nor separated by a double bar.[7] Furthermore, the crossed-out chords suggest that at one time Beethoven considered a reversal of the long–short rhythmic pattern used for the trumpet-like fanfare.

Ex. 53. Sketches for the second movement

The 'concept' sketch on p. 195, has an unusual layout. Beethoven's numbering directs that the sketch is to be read clockwise: we begin with Var. 1 on st. 6b, go upwards to sts. 4 and 5 for Vars. 2 and 3, and descend back to st. 6c for Var. 4 (Ex. 54a). It is tempting to hypothesize that Beethoven added these numbers only after he wrote the sketch, and realized that the low register of Vars. 1 and 4 provided an effective foil for the higher register of Vars. 2 and 3.

Not only does the overall tessitura organization in this sketch anticipate the final version, but the incipit for Var. 2 details the specific texture for that variation. The melody is now embedded in the sixteenth-note figuration (although in an inner voice rather than on the top) and shifted off the beat to the second or third sixteenth. As noted above, the pointed articulation pattern indicated here for Var. 2 was traded for a smoother effect. Beethoven thus ensured continuity

---

[7] Sketches survive for a similar tempo and dynamic bridge connecting the Adagio and Scherzo movements of Op. 96. These too make no distinction between the two movements. See Mary Rowen Obelkevich, 'The Growth of a Musical Idea— Beethoven's Opus 96', *Current Musicology*, 11 (1971), 103.

Ex. 54. Sketches for the second movement

by emphasizing the larger beat motion rather than micro-units of the beat. The melodic syncopation, which was retained, could then emerge in a less obtrusive way.

On the same page, another sketch for the connection between movements II and III confirms Beethoven was striving for the impression of an unbroken union (Ex. 54b). The striking upward leap that caps the Andante now appears unencumbered (although the leap is a sixth, rather than the octave found in the final version), followed by the rhythmic acceleration opening the finale.

The paucity of sketches for the finale imposes severe limitations on what we can learn; however, some aspects of its beginnings are anticipated in Beethoven's sketches for other works of this period. There is, for example, a piano sketch in C in the Kessler Sketchbook (fo. 189^v/sts. 13–14), probably intended for Op. 31, which opens with a turn figure similar to the one characterizing 1P.[8] A related motive also occurs on an earlier page of Mendelssohn 15, in the context of work on 'Nur hurtig fort', from *Leonore*.[9] Furthermore, two important structural procedures surface in a draft for Op. 31 No. 2/I: the idea of

---

[8] Bathia Churgin points out this relationship in her review of *Ludwig van Beethoven: Kesslersches Skizzenbuch*, p. 177 n. 7.

[9] Although the sketch is in A minor, the resemblance to the turn motive of Op. 57/III is clear, as mentioned in *N II*, p. 442.

using a closed binary form in the coda, with the tonal plan i–III–i; and the repetition of the development and the recapitulation.[10] Both of these ideas were rejected for Op. 31, but incorporated into the finale of Op. 57.

The earliest entry for the finale in Mendelssohn 15 shares certain general traits with the primary theme of the final version, such as a registral descent from high to low, a steady sixteenth-note motion that broadens out to punctuate the cadence, and an up-beat pattern in the cadential measures. Otherwise, its opening figuration bears more resemblance to the étude style Beethoven had adopted for the finale of Op. 54. In particular, the texture—a dominant pedal on top with the melody emerging from the underlying sixteenths—recalls the primary theme in that movement. We can surmise Beethoven rejected it here for pianistic reasons, since the large skips in the theme would make it difficult to play at a rapid tempo (Ex. 55).

Ex. 55. An early sketch for the third movement

The three remaining entries focus on the tempo bridge introducing the primary theme of the third movement. A sketch on p. 191/ sts. 4c–5 approximates mm. 6–20 of the finale, although it is four measures shorter (Ex. 56a). Beethoven would later add more pattern repetitions, and extend the musical space by descending to the lowest octave of his piano.

On a lower portion of the same page Beethoven sketched the opening fanfare (Ex. 56b). Again, the rhythmic plan shows an eighth-note preceding the first dotted-quarter. We can surmise Beethoven eventually eliminated this up-beat because it weakens the percussive impact of the first chord.[11] In contrast, when placed on the down-beat,

[10] As pointed out in Cooper, 'The Origins of Beethoven's D Minor Sonata Op. 31 No. 2', pp. 261–80.

[11] Paul Mies shows how in many instances Beethoven added up-beats to themes that were originally begun on the down-beat. Here we see the process working in

Ex. 56. Sketches for the opening, third movement

the dotted-quarter articulates the sudden shift in mood, while simultaneously providing a smoother departure from the sustained half-notes closing the Andante. Although there is no suggestion that the repeated eighth-notes are to be dotted (as in mm. 3–4 of the final version), the sustained pedal indication is already in place. The concluding part of the sketch drafts the link into 1P; here, the melodic profile suddenly rises to c′, before returning to the lower register for the theme. Eventually, Beethoven retained the low register for the end of the introduction, saving the peak of c′ to highlight the actual entrance of the theme (m. 20 in the final version).

The last entry (Ex. 57) still retains the up-beat form of the fanfare, but the ff shattering the tranquillity of the Andante is in place, as is the turn figure locking the end of the introduction into the beginning of 1P.

These fragments—clearly remnants of what must have been a much more detailed process of evolution—are valuable for their testimony regarding Beethoven's priorities at this stage. For the Andante these were the need to ensure a logical, smooth progression between the

reverse. See Mies, *Beethoven's Sketches: An Analysis of his Style Based on a Study of his Sketchbooks*, trans. Doris L. Mackinnon (London, 1929; repr. New York, 1974), 1–16.

Ex. 57. Sketch for the opening, third movement

variations, and the desire to imbue this essentially additive form with a sense of seamless flow. For the finale it was the shaping of the join between the two movements (another facet of the same issue) that concerned him.

Because all of the surviving finale sketches, with the exception of the earliest one, focus on this connective passage, it is possible that they stem from a later developmental stage than the sketches for the other movements. If, in fact, Beethoven had already made substantial progress on the finale elsewhere, perhaps on loose sheets that have not survived, he could have returned to these few empty spaces in Mendelssohn 15 to refine this pivotal point in the sonata's structure.

PART IV.   THE AUTOGRAPH

9. Overview and Revisions in the Finale

OVERVIEW

The autograph of Op. 57 is currently housed in the Bibliothèque Nationale in Paris (catalogued as Manuscript 20). At one time it was the property of the pianist, Marie Bigot, and the way in which she acquired the manuscript has become one of the better-known stories in the literature. Marie's husband relates that, in the autumn of 1806, Beethoven went on a trip to Prince Lichnowsky's residence in Gratz, near Troppau.[1] The two men quarrelled and Beethoven returned prematurely to Vienna.[2] During the journey there was a severe storm and the autograph of Op. 57, which Beethoven had packed in his trunk, became water-stained.[3] Later, while carrying the manuscript to his publisher, the Bureau des Arts et d'Industrie, Beethoven stopped at the Bigots. As Monsieur Bigot states:

After reaching Vienna, [Beethoven] came to see us and laughingly showed the work, which was still wet, to my wife, who at once began to look carefully at it. Impelled by the striking beginning she sat down at the pianoforte and began playing it. Beethoven had not expected this and was surprised to note that Madame Bigot did not hesitate at all because of the many erasures and alterations which he had made. It was the original manuscript which he was carrying to his publisher for printing. When Mme. Bigot finished playing she begged him to give it to her; he consented, and faithfully brought it to her after it had been printed.[4]

---

[1] *Thayer's Life of Beethoven*, ed. Forbes, p. 407, reports that M. Bigot's story was written half a century after the event, 'on a printed copy of the sonata belonging to the pianist Mortier de Fontaine'.

[2] For the dating of Beethoven's return to Vienna, see his letters, Anderson Nos. 134 and 136. The former, dated 3 Sept. 1806, was written from Silesia; the latter, dated 1 Nov. 1806, was written from Vienna. Another letter from Breuning to Wegeler, written in October, suggests it was Beethoven's intention to stay in Silesia until the end of the month (see *Thayer's life of Beethoven*, ed. Forbes, p. 402); thus, Beethoven's hasty departure probably took place in the second half of October.

[3] Water-staining in Op. 57/I and II, and on the autograph of Op. 59 No. 2, as well as on sketches for the third and fourth movements of this quartet and for Op. 59 No. 3/I, probably also occurred at this same time. See Tyson, 'The "Razumovsky" Quartets', p. 129.

[4] Quoted from *Thayer's Life of Beethoven*, ed. Forbes, p. 407.

The sonata was published on 21 February 1807, so Marie would have received it sometime around this date. This gift, together with several letters written by Beethoven to Marie and her husband in March 1807, have caused some speculation that Beethoven might have had some romantic feelings for Marie.[5] It is equally likely however, that Beethoven simply regarded Marie and her family as 'dear friends, in whose company he could experience the family warmth lacking in his own solitary existence'.[6]

In 1809 the Bigots moved to Paris, where, until her death in 1820, Marie was a professional performer and teacher.[7] In 1852 her husband gave the autograph to the pianist René Paul Baillot.[8] René presented the autograph to the Paris Conservatory in 1889, and from there it passed to its present home in the Bibliothèque Nationale. There are two modern facsimile editions of the autograph: an edition by H. Piazza (Paris, 1927), and the recent reissue of the Paris edition by Peters (Leipzig, 1970).

We do not know precisely when Beethoven copied out the autograph of Op. 57, but the watermark of its paper provides a clue. We find two different paper-types, both of which have twelve staves and are in oblong format, with each page measuring approximately 218 × 305 mm. The total span of the staves in paper-type I is 185 mm. The watermark consists of three half-moons on the border between quadrants 3 and 4; quadrant 2 is empty and quadrants 1 and 4 contain the following: FS/G.A. EMERICH. There are two moulds; only mould A is used for the autograph. In paper-type II the total span of the staves is 185 + to 185.5 mm. The watermark consists of three half-moons in quadrant 3; quadrants 1 and 4 are empty, and quadrant 2 contains the initials FS. As with paper-type I, the moulds are similar. Only two leaves are paper-type I, and in fact the two types are so similar that they may be variants of each other.[9]

---

[5] The letters concerned are Anderson Nos. 138, 138a, and 139. See also *Thayer's Life of Beethoven*, ed. Forbes, pp. 413–15.

[6] This interpretation is from Maynard Solomon, *Beethoven* (New York, 1977), 81.

[7] For biographical information on Marie Bigot, see F. J. Fétis, *Biographie universelle des musiciens* (2nd edn., Paris, 1866), i. 413; and also Hugh Macdonald, 'Marie Bigot', in *The New Grove Dictionary of Music and Musicians*, ii. 701.

[8] See René Baillot, *Le Ménestrel* (Sunday, 18 July 1880), 261–2. René's father, a celebrated violin teacher at the Paris conservatory, met Beethoven in Vienna in 1805 (see Kinsky–Halm, p. 135).

[9] Information on both paper-types comes from Tyson, 'The "Razumovsky" Quartets', pp. 109–12 (my paper-type I is Tyson's Paper 2, and my type II is his Paper 1). The watermark of paper-type II is catalogued by Joseph Schmidt-Görg as No. 86 in 'Die Wasserzeichen in Beethoven's Notenpapieren', in Kurt Dorfmüller (ed.)

Both papers were also used for the autograph of Op. 59 No. 1, inscribed by Beethoven with the remark 'angefangen am 26ten Mai 1806'. Alan Tyson suggests that Beethoven began using this paper in 'the spring or early summer of 1806', and he believes that the autograph of Op. 57 dates from around this time.[10]

Turning our investigation now to the outward appearance of the manuscript, we see it consists of forty-four pages, forty-two of which contain notation, with two blank pages appearing at the end. An outline of the gathering structure is provided in Table 12. The three stab holes found on the inner margin of each page, as well as the

TABLE 12. *The gathering structure of the autograph (Bibliothèque Nationale, MS 20)*

Page	Paper	Quadrant	Page	Paper	Quadrant
1/2	I	4A	23/24	II	3A
3/4	II	4A	25/26	II	4A
5/6	II	3A	27/28	II	1A
7/8	II	4A	29/30	II	2A
9/10	II	2A			
11/12	II	1A	31/32	II	4B
13/14	II	3A	33/34	II	3B
15/16	II	1A	35/36	II	2B
17/18	II	2A	37/38	II	1B
19/20	II	1A			
21/22	I	1A	39/40	II	2A
			41/42	II	1A
			43/44	II	4A

Note:
The outline of the gathering structure was kindly provided by Sieghard Brandenburg.

Beiträge zur Beethoven Bibliographie: Studien und Materialien zum Werkverzeichnis von Kinsky-Halm (Munich, 1978), 173.

[10] See Alan Tyson, 'In questa tomba oscura', in Harry Goldschmidt (ed.), *Bericht über den Internationalen Beethoven-Kongress Berlin 1977* (Leipzig, 1978), 241, for information that the following sources also use paper-type II: the autograph of Op. 59 No. 2./I (Mendelssohn 10 in the Staatsbibliothek Preussischer Kulturbesitz, Berlin); an autograph of the arietta 'In questa tomba oscura', WoO 133 (in the Memorial Library of Music at Stanford University, Ca.); a fragment of a rejected score for the Fourth Symphony (Landsberg 12, pp. 53–6, in the Deutsche Staatsbibliothek, Berlin); and some excerpts from Handel's *Messiah*, copied by Beethoven (Landsberg 10, pp. 57–64, in the Staatsbibliothek Preussischer Kulturbesitz, Berlin). Tyson states that 'all of these autographs can be dated with some confidence to the spring, summer or autumn of 1806'.

reinforcing strip of paper at the end of the first and third gatherings, show that the present binding is not the original one; perhaps it was added by the Bigots.

The manuscript displays marked evidence of water damage. The pale, tan pages are frequently blotched with dark stains, particularly on the edges. In some instances, there are holes torn in the outer margins (see pp. 21/22, st. 6; pp. 27/28, st. 8, for example). Certain pages appear to have been so badly damaged that a white strip of matching paper has been added to prevent further tearing. In addition, the first three staves and part of the fourth and fifth staves on pp. 19/20 have been cut out and replaced by an insert in an unidentified hand.[11] Unfortunately, the rewritten measures corrupt the text for the penultimate section of the coda in the first movement (mm. 249–52 and 256). It is clear that the copyist misunderstood the rhythm in mm. 251–4; besides errors in the notes, he divided m. 251 into two, and added extra notes in m. 254.[12] Similarly, he introduced errors in the first section of the theme in the second movement: in m. 5 the *sfp* has been replaced by *fp*, and in m. 8 the right-hand chord is misspelt (F–Ab–Db, instead of Db–F–Db). The first edition does not duplicate these particular mistakes, so we can assume that the interpolation occurred after the manuscript was used by the engraver.

We know that Beethoven generally preferred to have the engraver work from his own autograph rather than from a copyist's score, because he felt this produced the most accurate results.[13] It is also possible that he feared recopying would either cause him to introduce more careless errors, or tempt him to make further changes.[14] Ample proof that the autograph of Op. 57 served as the *Stichvorlage* occurs in several places. The plate number '521' for the printing of the first edition appears on the first page; 'x' marks (usually between staves) denoting page turns are visible on pp. 4, 7, 11, 13, 17, 19, 23, 30, 33, 35, and 38; and in several instances there are numbers corresponding to page numbers in the first edition.[15] Periodically, editorial marks in

[11] This insertion was probably made to compensate for the damage due to water-staining. See Kinsky–Halm, p. 134.

[12] For a detailed discussion of the mistakes in these measures, see Anneliese Leicher-Olbrich, *Untersuchungen zu Originalausgaben Beethovenscher Klavierwerke* (Wiesbaden, 1976), 215–16.   [13] See Anderson No. 220.

[14] As suggested in Alan Tyson, 'Steps to Publication and Beyond', in Denis Arnold and Nigel Fortune (eds.) *The Beethoven Companion* (London, 1971), 467. As Tyson points out, Opp. 28, 33, 34, 35, and 53 were all engraved from Beethoven's autograph (p. 468).

[15] See Leicher-Olbrich, *Untersuchungen*, p. 217. Numbers corresponding to pages in the first edition appear on pp. 4, 7, 11, 13, 17, 19, and 23 of the autograph. These numbers are most easily seen in the H. Piazza edition.

red crayon designate excisions (for example, pp. 39–40), the in-corporation of missing notes (for example, p. 3, second system, left hand), accidentals (pp. 7, 28, 32, 38, and 39), and pedal markings (for example, p. 17).

On most pages Beethoven has left every third stave free (pp. 2 and 37 are exceptions).[16] The desire to leave room for potential changes was probably behind this writing pattern, and may also account for the large-sized measures, often only two or three to each system (this is most prevalent in the first movement; see, for example, p. 2).[17]

With this general picture in mind, let us now try to discover to what extent the autograph of Op. 57 functioned as part of the compositional process.

REVISIONS IN THE FINALE

There is increasing evidence that an intimate relationship between sketches and autograph exists in Beethoven.[18] A study of the Op. 57 autograph reinforces this assumption. In this case, Beethoven's most significant revisions take place in the finale, and therefore I have confined my remarks to specific passages in this movement.[19] Beethoven's alterations here affect every musical element, and, although none of them modifies basic structural relationships, they do offer valuable insights concerning his working procedures.[20]

In the following discussion I have organized my comments under the classifications of Sound, Rhythm, and Growth. For the identification

[16] See Lockwood, 'On Beethoven's Sketches and Autographs', p. 37. Lockwood points out that, among the published autographs of the piano sonatas, the spacing for Op. 57 is unique; Opp. 26, 27 No. 2, 53, 78, 109, 110, and 111 are written on eight-stave paper, with all the staves on each page filled in. The autograph of Op. 28 (unpublished, in the Beethovenhaus in Bonn) follows the pattern of the majority.

[17] As suggested in Alan Tyson, 'Stages in the Composition of Beethoven's Piano Trio Op. 70 No. I', *Proceedings of the Royal Musical Association*, 97 (1970–1), 15.

[18] For the importance of Beethoven's revisions in the autograph stage, see the valuable studies by Lewis Lockwood, 'The Autograph of the First Movement of Beethoven's Sonata for Violoncello and Pianoforte, Op. 69', in *The Music Forum*, ii, ed. William Mitchell and Felix Salzer (New York, 1970), 1–109; and Tyson, 'Stages in the Composition of Beethoven's Piano Trio Op. 70 No. 1'.

[19] An outline of variants in all three movements appears in Edmund Schmid, 'Beethovens *Appassionata*: Ein Vergleich zwischen Autograph und Drucktexten', *Schweizerische Musikzeitung*, 79 (1939), 161–6. For the first movement, see the more recent comparison by Leicher-Olbrich, *Untersuchungen*, pp. 213–405.

[20] For an understanding of how Beethoven's reworking could affect the overall impact of a composition, see Janet M. Levy, *Beethoven's Compositional Choices: The Two Versions of Op. 18 No. 1, First Movement* (Philadelphia, 1982). This study compares two finished versions, but the same principles can be applied to revisions within a single autograph.

of the sonata-form functions, *P*, *T*, *S*, *K*, etc., the reader is referred to the analysis of the final version, Chapter 3.

Sound

1. *Changes in register*
In the exposition, three different arrangements of the transition area (mm. 64–73) are discernible (the alterations begin in m. 68; see Fig. 4). Beethoven's revisions here acquire more meaning if we recall that the registers of his piano sounded more heterogeneous than those of the modern instrument: the highest had a thin, flute-like quality, while the middle was more mellow.[21] In the first version of this passage Beethoven maintained the high register for mm. 64–9, dropped lower for mm. 70–1, and returned to the higher level for the final part of the function. As a second thought, he placed the registral descent in an earlier position (note the crossed-out 'Vi:' entered above m. 68 and the writing of the right hand of mm. 68–9 in the lower octave on st. 3, marked '= de'). Finally, he sustained the higher register in the right hand for the whole passage (indicated by 'bleibt' above mm. 68–9, 'in 8va' above mm. 70–1, and 'loco' over mm. 72–3). This choice integrates the entire transition and makes its sound more penetrating. In addition, because it eliminates registral contrast within the melodic line of *T*, the subsequent rise in the left hand becomes more audible (mm. 74–5), highlighting the entrance of the second theme.

2. *Changes in dynamics*
There is a small dynamic change in the exposition, where the crescendo originally marked in m. 58 was replaced by a forte. This intensification brings the climactic effect of $2P^1$ (mm. 50–63) into sharper focus; the revision also stands in the parallel passage in the recapitulation.

A more substantial change occurs in the closing area, where Beethoven crossed out the *sf* indications under the final chords of each phrase in the right hand, but retained them for the up-beat beginning each phrase (see the autograph, mm. 102, 104, 106, 108, 110, and the parallel measures in the recapitulation). By restricting these dynamic accents to the beginning of the phrase, Beethoven imposes a syncopated phrase pattern on the right hand that contrasts with the down-beat

---

[21] On the special qualities of the Viennese pianos that Beethoven is thought to have preferred, see William S. Newman, 'Beethoven's Piano versus his Piano Ideals', *Journal of the American Musicological Society*, 23 (1970), 498. Additional information on the tone quality of the fortepiano in Beethoven's time is found in Rosenblum, *Performance Practices*, pp. 37–8.

phrase pattern in the left hand.[22] The resolution of this dissonant effect in m. 112, with the synchronization of down-beat stress in both hands reinforced by *ff* and pedal indications, now stands out more prominently, signalling the link into the development.

Rhythm

1. *Changes in the surface rhythm*
A revision in the final measure of the retransition (m. 211) shows that initially Beethoven maintained continuity with mm. 206–10 by sustaining the half-note rhythm in the left hand; later, he substituted the syncopated pattern of the final version. This improved the passage in two ways: it sharpened the structural frame, by giving impetus to the beginning of the recapitulation; and it provided a subtle integrative touch, by recalling an important up-beat pattern from the left hand of the primary theme (see mm. 21–2, 23–4, and 25–6 in the exposition, which do not recur in the recapitulation).

A famous textural problem centres around the tie between beats one and two: it does not appear in the first edition, although it is quite clear in the autograph. It is possible that this tie was mistakenly omitted by the engraver, because it is reinstated in the Moscheles edition of 1837.[23]

Another rhythmic change occurs in the transition area of the recapitulation (mm. 266–7), where Beethoven rewrote the last beat in m. 266 and both beats in m. 267 as eighths rather than sixteenths. This creates a more gradual deceleration into the slower values in the left hand of m. 268, and avoids the excessive repetition of db^2 that anticipates the first melodic note of S. Furthermore, it calls attention to the reworking of the harmonic procedure here: whereas in the exposition the Neapolitan harmony initiating S is preceded by its tonic (thereby echoing the primary theme), in the recapitulation the Neapolitan is approached by means of its dominant (Ex. 58).

Growth

1. *Recasting of the new theme in the development (*1N*, mm. 142–58)*
Massive recomposition occurs on p. 31 of the autograph, where, beneath the heavy tangle of revisions, a prior version of $1N$ emerges

[22] To ensure a sharp detachment at the end of the right-hand phrases, Beethoven has placed staccato strokes over the down-beats in mm. 104, 106, 108, and 110. These strokes do not appear in the first edition.

[23] The Moscheles edition of 1837 for Cramer & Co. is based on the Czerny edition for Haslinger of 1828–32, first issue. See Alan Tyson, 'Moscheles and his "Complete Edition" of Beethoven', *Music Review*, 25 (1964), 139.

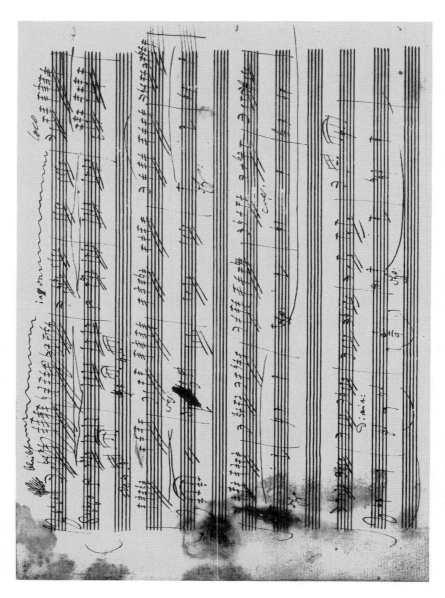

FIG. 4. Third movement autograph (Bibliothèque Nationale, MS 20), p. 28

Ex. 58. Autograph, third movement, mm. 266–7, first version

(Ex. 59; Fig. 5). A comparison of the initial layer with the final theme suggests that Beethoven was seeking a more integrated effect. In both cases the theme consists of two phrases (*a* and *b*), but in the final version the profile of the second phrase derives from the first, rather than contrasting with it. The gradual registral polarization marking the contrasting phrase *b* in the earlier attempt was then reserved for the retransition (mm. 168–75); in this way Beethoven sharpened the distinction between these two structural areas. He also enriched the texture of both phrases, so that a mirror relationship results between the two hands. At the same time motivic saturation is increased, as the changes create a simultaneous combination of the neighbour-tone motive (in mirror), with a falling third (in mm. 145–6 and 149–50, on F–Eb–Db; and in mm. 153–4 and 157–8, on C–Bb–Ab). This falling-third motive recalls *1K* in the first movement, and anticipates a later occurrence in the coda of the finale (see mm. 309–11, on Ab–G–F in the right hand).[24] The additional differences between the two versions of this theme (outlined in Table 13) show how Beethoven strengthened the impact of this section.

2. Compression of the primary theme area in the recapitulation

Two crossed-out measures at the top of p. 34 in the autograph suggest that originally Beethoven planned to parallel the exposition and begin the recapitulation from *1P*; the excised thirds in the left hand of mm. 3–6 on the same page imply that, on second thoughts, he decided to start from the ornamented repeat of the theme, *1P¹*. Finally, he telescoped the two sections, thereby making space for a new, eight-measure variant (mm. 220–7 in the final version). This solution enabled him to achieve a fresh effect while simultnaeously retaining the same proportions for the primary-theme area.[25]

---

[24] On the role of this falling-third motive, see Schenker's analysis, 'Beethoven: Sonata Opus 57'.

[25] It is also possible that Beethoven was writing so rapidly that he mistakenly copied out the exposition form, crossed it out, and made the corrections. But a similar

Ex. 59. Autograph, third movement, first version of 1N

3. The final segment of the coda

There are two main points of revision in the coda. The first concerns the last measure on p. 39 and the first measure on p. 40 of the autograph: excisions in red crayon show that, in this recall of the primary theme, Beethoven cancelled two extra measures of the Neapolitan

type of revision occurs in the second version of Op. 18 No. 1/I; see Levy, *Beethoven's Compositional Choices*, pp. 79–82.

TABLE 13. *Theme 1N, third movement (mm. 142–58): First and final versions compared*

First version	Final version
Phrase structure is symmetrical: $a–b$, $a^1–b^1$ Intensification in phrases b and b^1 is effected by a thicker texture and lower register.	Phraseology is more developmental: $a–a^1$, $b–b^1$ Intensification is effected by a rise in register, integrating 1N with other themes in the movement. See, for example, P, where 2P encompasses a higher register than 1P; T, where Beethoven decided to sustain a high register for the whole section; and K, where registral ascents intensify phrase repetitions.
The harmony is more diffuse and less goal-directed because Beethoven alternates the keys. Phrase: $a–b$, $a^1–b^1$ Harmony: b♭–f, b♭–f	The harmony is more directional because the goal of F minor is saved for the second half of the function: Phrase: $a–a^1$, $b–b^1$ Harmony: b♭ f
The theme seems rhythmically and melodically static; the duplication in phrase b of the one-measure rhythmic pattern originating in phrase a produces seven repetitions in a row.	The phrase rhythm avoids excessive repetition of one-measure rhythmic patterns.

harmony. This may actually have been a simple correction of a copying error; but, because the right hand in the second measure on p. 40 begins the Neapolitan pattern from b♭ rather than from g♭', the additional measures may have been intentional.[26]

The second area of revision is more comprehensive (Ex. 60; Fig. 6). Several different types of alterations occur here. Small changes in harmony and rhythm, for example, strengthen the impact of mm. 341–8. In the first version the top note in the left-hand tonic chord is the fifth, C, a tone that tends to be passive, since it is common

[26] Elimination of repetitions is a type of revision found elsewhere in Beethoven's autograph scores. See, for example, Benito V. Rivera, 'Rhythmic Organization in Beethoven's Seventh Symphony', *19th-Century Music*, 6 (1983), 241–51.

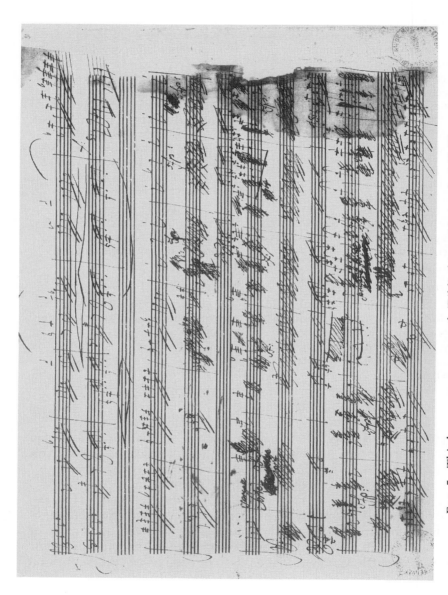

FIG. 5.   Third movement autograph (Bibliothèque Nationale, MS 20), p. 31

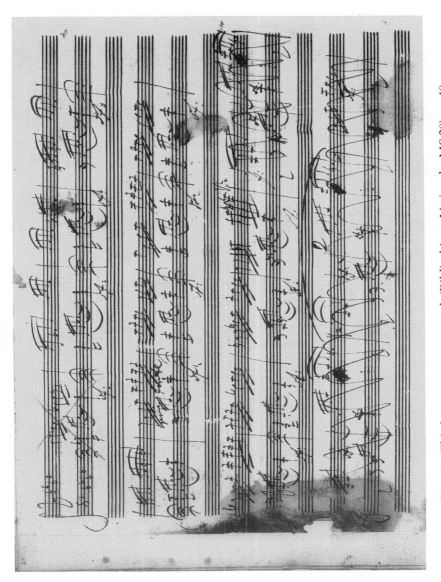

Fig. 6. Third movement autograph (Bibliothèque Nationale, MS 20), p. 40

Ex. 60. Autograph, third movement, first version of mm. 341 ff.

to both the tonic and dominant chords; in the final version this note becomes the more active third, Ab. Because both hands now emphasize this pitch with an *sf* indication, the melodic imitation between the two voices becomes more audible. Rhythmically, Beethoven shortened the up-beat in the left hand, thus intensifying the impact of the modular acceleration that occurs in these measures.

Beethoven also recast the registral plan. In the first version mm. 341–52 are mostly in the middle range; there follow a sudden rise and then a descent, so that the melodic profile recalls the diffuse contour found in the last six measures of the first movement. In the final version Beethoven begins an octave higher, then plunges headlong into a more-than-four-octave descent; as a result, he was able to compress the action by two measures (the ascent to c^4 in the first version of mm. 353–4 was eliminated), and embue the entire passage with a powerful, downward directional force.

Additional tightening resulted from excising the three measures of rest punctuating each of the three final chords. This last change permits momentum gathered in the closing measures to escalate beyond the cadence.[27] A strikingly similar revision appears during Beethoven's work on the first movement of the Violin Sonata, Op. 30 No. 2. A comparison of a sketch for the end of this movement found on fo. 56^r/sts. 15–16 of the Kessler Sketchbook with mm. 253–4 of the final version shows that, whereas the sketch allows three full measures for the closing chords, the final version contracts this to two measures.

In summary, we can see that numerous compositional changes, particularly for the development and coda of the finale, take place in the autograph. The changes range from modest adjustments in registral planning and harmonies to major recasting of themes. But, whatever their scope, such refinements both enlarge our understanding of Beethoven's working methods, and attest to his drive to perfect every aspect of this music.

[27] The fermatas above the last rests in the autograph do not appear in the first edition nor in the Moscheles and Schenker editions, but are restored in the Henle–Wallner edition. The transcription given in Ex. 60 appears in Alfred Einstein, 'Neuausgaben alter Musikwerke', *Zeitschrift für Musikwissenschaft*, 10 (1927–8), 62, with the exception of the following: Einstein does not transcribe the first layer of m. 340 and he omits the forte indication in the penultimate measure.

PART V. TRANSCRIPTIONS AND FACSIMILES

10. Preface

All the sketches for the 'Appassionata' found in Mendelssohn 15 are transcribed in Chapter 11. Since no facsimile edition of the sketchbook has yet been published, I have included facsimiles of each page as Chapter 12. This will allow the reader an opportunity to view the excerpts found as examples in the body of the text in their original context and format, and to compare the transcriptions with the originals.

The transcription procedures seek to facilitate ease of reading and intelligibility. While Beethoven's original beaming has been retained, placement of notes on the stave as well as direction of stems have been regularized. Editorial clefs, rests, and accidentals have been added where necessary and placed in square brackets; in the case of editorial stems, ties, barlines, or beams, dotted lines are generally used. Other editorial additions or remarks appear in parentheses. Time signatures have not been supplied, because they are usually clear. Where the reading is doubtful, there is a question mark. In those instances where more than one layer of sketching appears, the layers have been separated and the different versions indicated. In a few cases I have arranged the transcription so that it reflects the musical continuity rather than the exact placement on the page (see, for example, p. 187/sts. 5b–10b, an early sketch for the secondary theme). Arrows refer to connections between sketches.

The only other published transcription of these sketches is by Gustav Nottebohm.[1] While Nottebohm's transcriptions are perceptive, they are selective, and therefore omit most of the material presented here. Nottebohm's selectivity is understandable, as many of the sketches are very difficult to decipher. In those cases where Beethoven's handwriting does not permit an unambiguous solution, I have tried to base my interpretation on musical grounds. Thus, for example, the sketch for the cadence in the first movement, p. 189/st. 9, mm. 15–16, is transcribed entirely in the treble clef because the pitches make the most sense this way, even though Beethoven's treble-clef sign after

---

[1] See *N II*, pp. 437–41. Nottebohm's transcriptions are copied in Jacques Gabriel Prod'homme, *Les Sonates pour piano de Beethoven* (Paris, 1937), 173–5; however, Prod'homme mistakenly includes a sketch for Op. 81a/II on p. 175 (the sketch is found in *N II*, p. 99).

the first two notes suggests an opening in the bass clef. In those instances where more than one solution is logical, my choice has been determined by both the context of the sketch and a cumulative feeling for Beethoven's intention, deriving from my study of all the sketches for this work.

11. Transcriptions

Transcription of Mendelssohn 15, p. 182

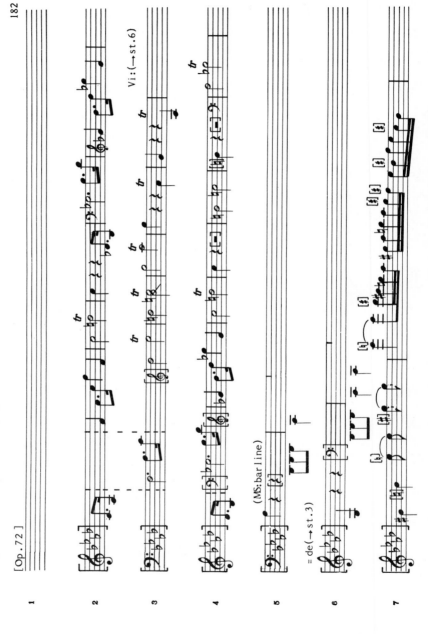

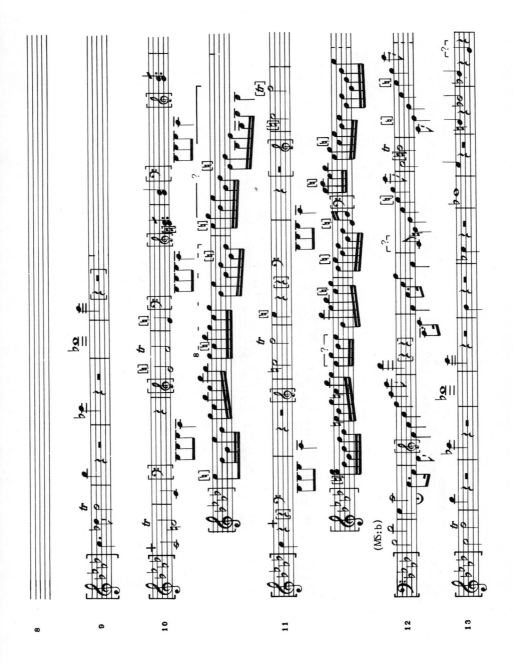

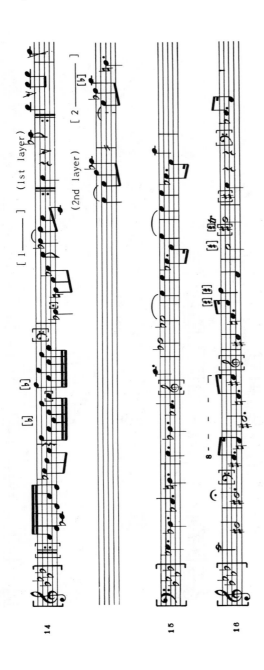

Transcription of Mendelssohn 15, p. 187

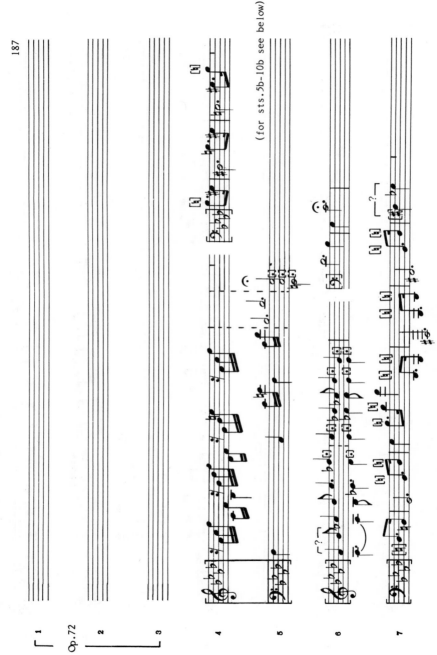

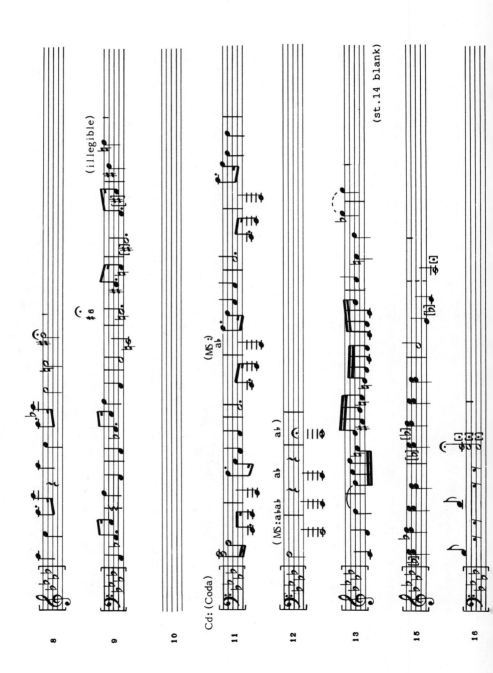

Transcription of Mendelssohn 15, p. 187, sts. 5b–10b

Transcription of Mendelssohn 15, p. 188

(st.16 blank)

Transcription of Mendelssohn 15, p. 189

12

13

14

15

16

Transcription of Mendelssohn 15, p. 190

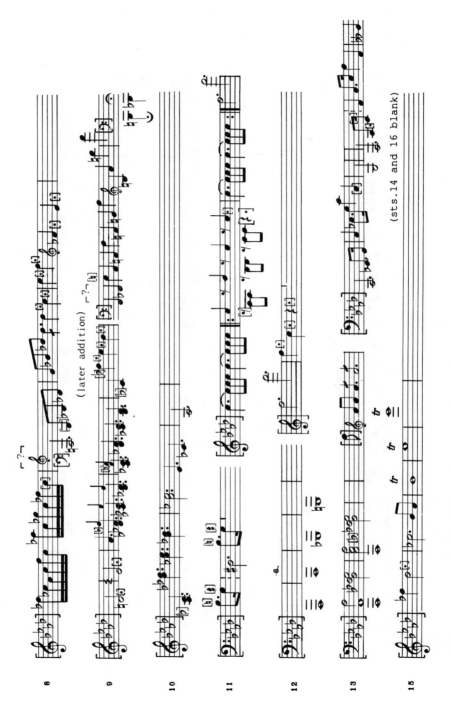

(later addition)

(sts.14 and 16 blank)

8

9

10

11

12

13

15

Transcription of Mendelssohn 15, p. 191

Ultimo pezzo

191

8va ?

8 - - - -

etc.

1

2

3

4

5

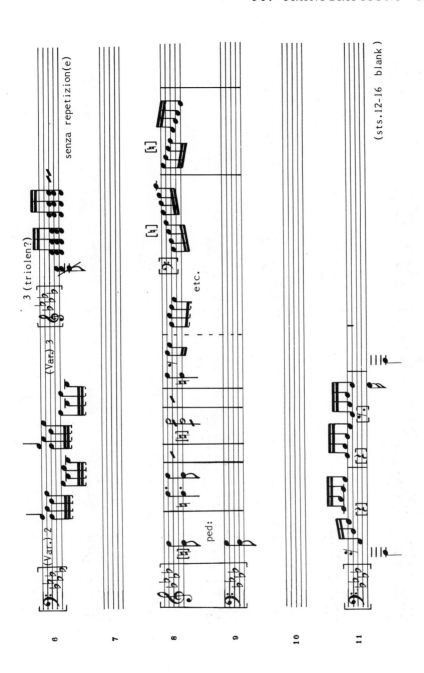

Transcription of Mendelssohn 15, p. 192

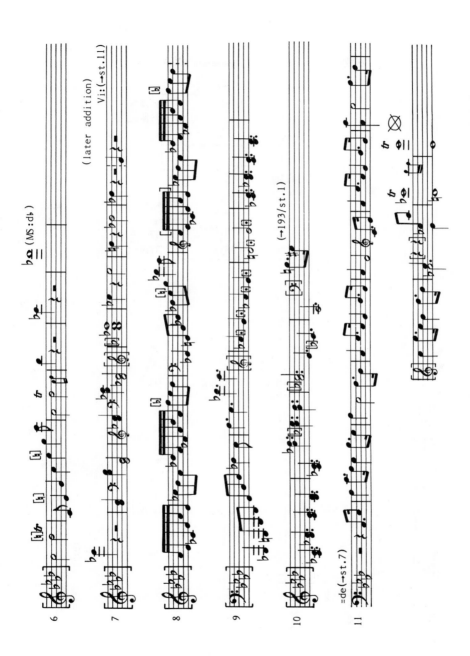

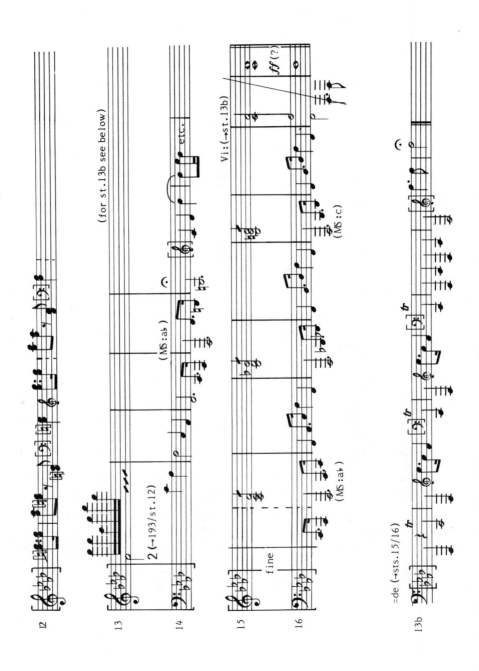

Transcription of Mendelssohn 15, p. 193

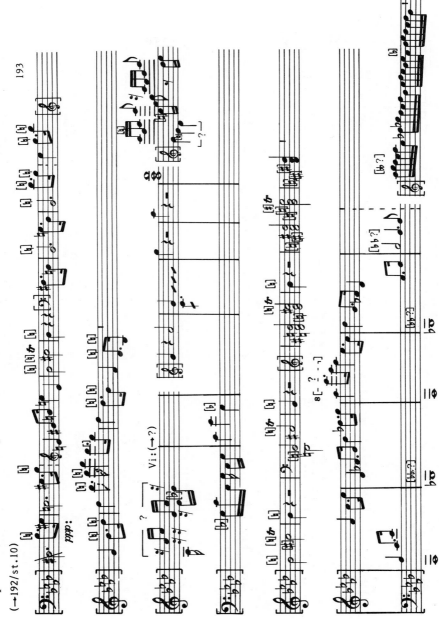

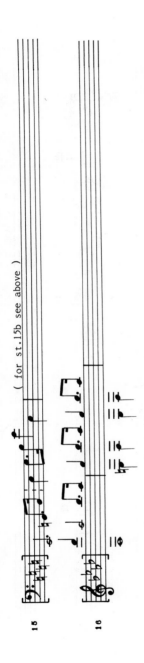

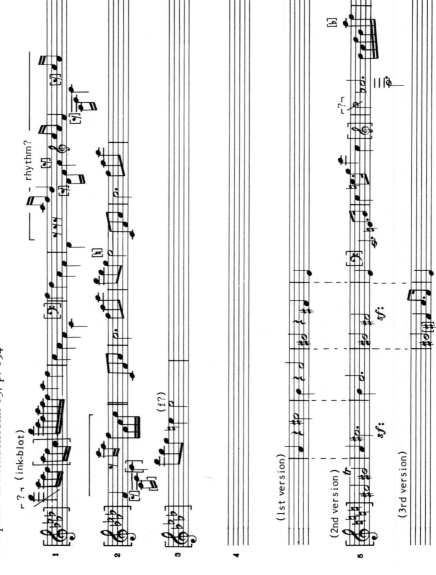

Transcription of Mendelssohn 15, p. 194

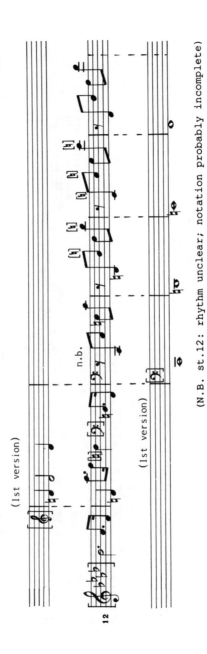

(N.B. st.12: rhythm unclear; notation probably incomplete)

Transcription of Mendelssohn 15, p. 195

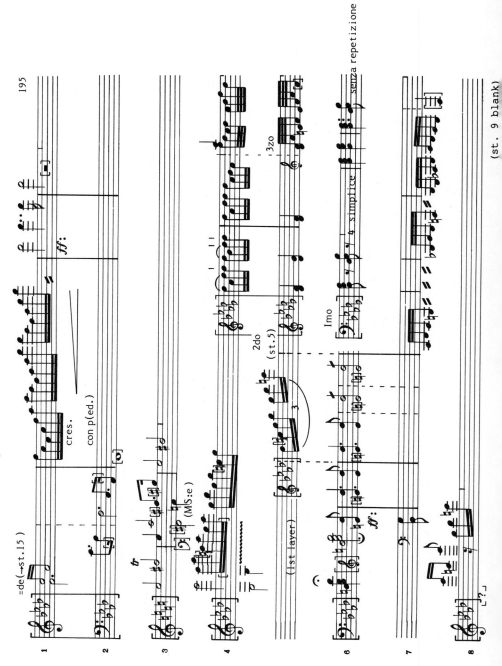

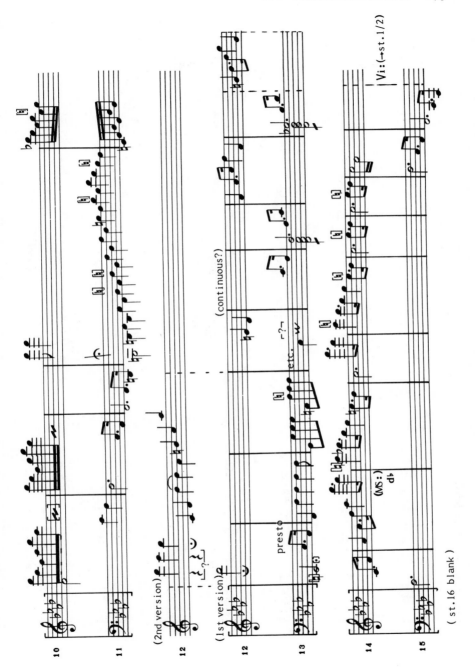

Transcription of Mendelssohn 15, p. 196

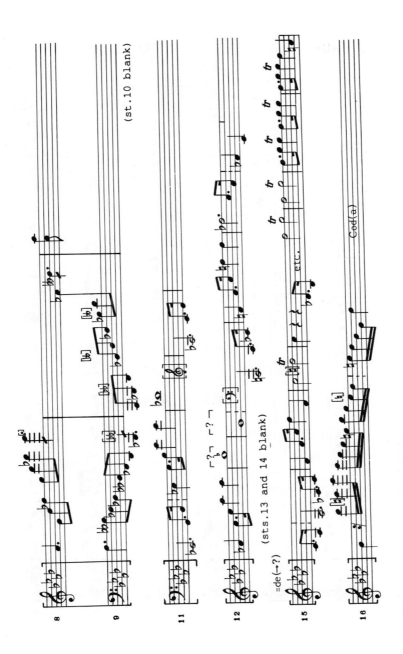

Transcription of Mendelssohn 15, p. 197

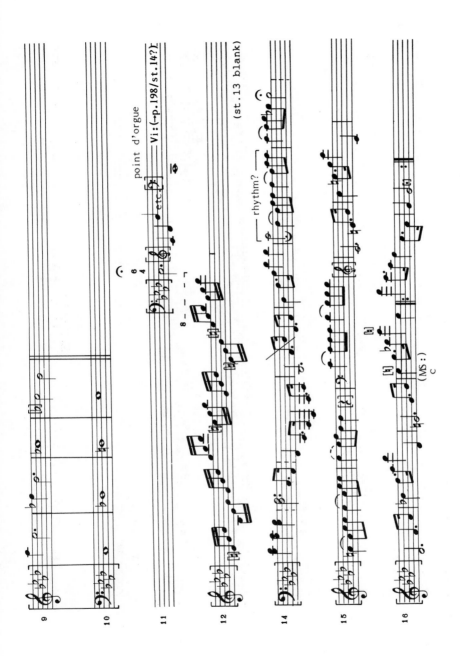

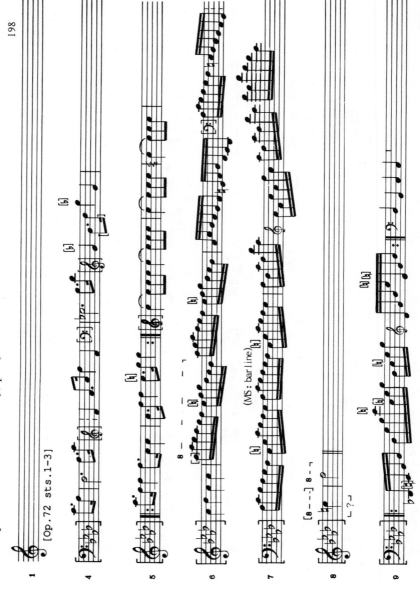

Transcription of Mendelssohn 15, p. 198

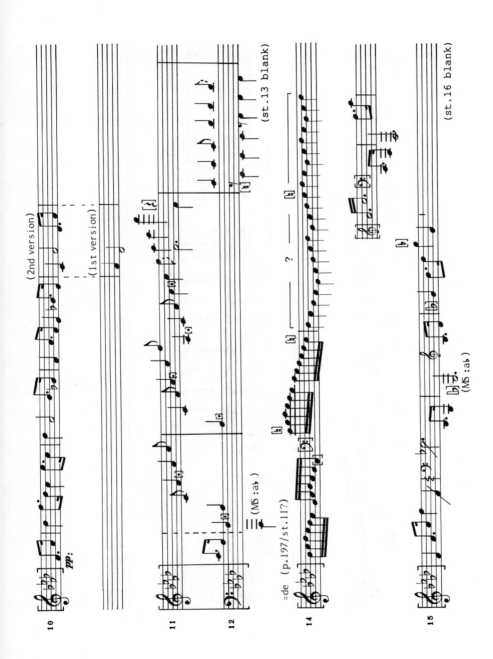

Transcription of Mendelssohn 15, p. 203

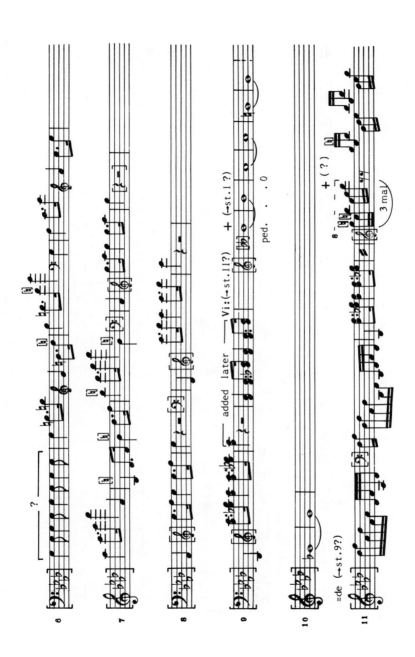

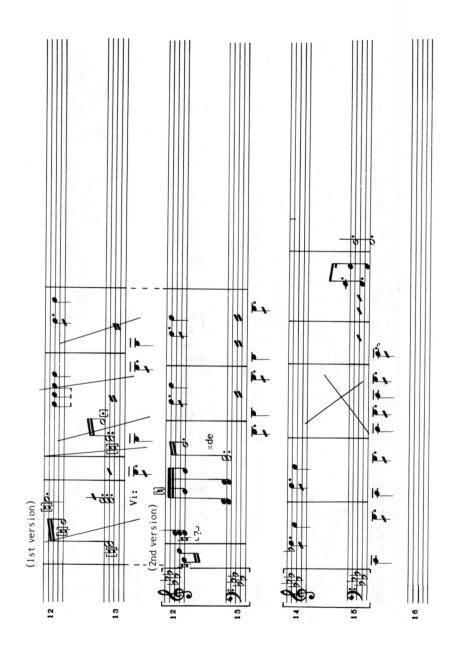

12.   *Facsimiles*

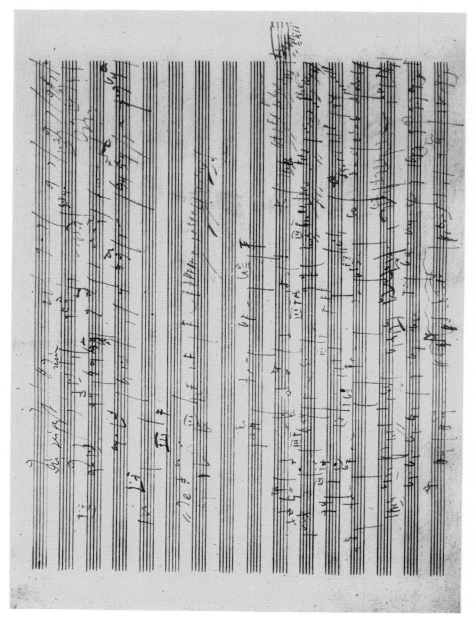

Facsimile of Mendelssohn 15, p. 182

Facsimile of Mendelssohn 15, p. 187

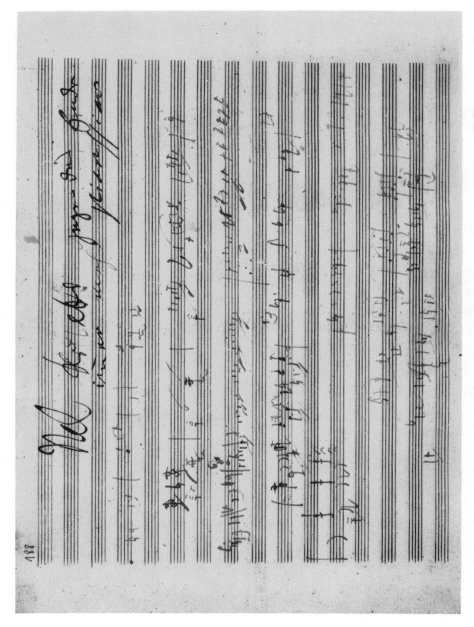

Facsimile of Mendelssohn 15, p. 188

Facsimile of Mendelssohn 15, p. 189

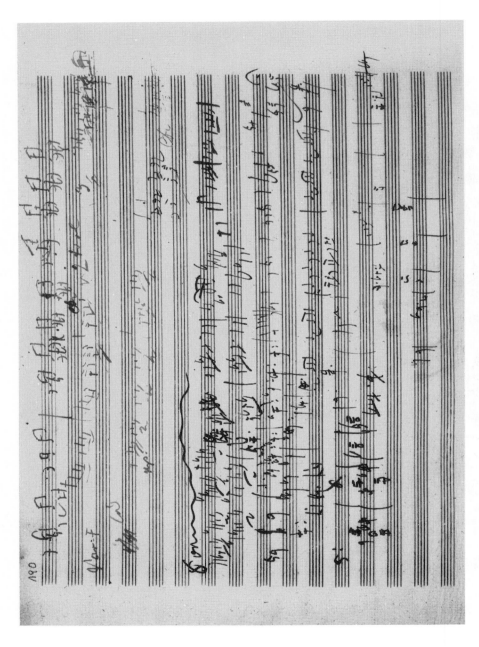

Facsimile of Mendelssohn 15, p. 190

Facsimile of Mendelssohn 15, p. 191

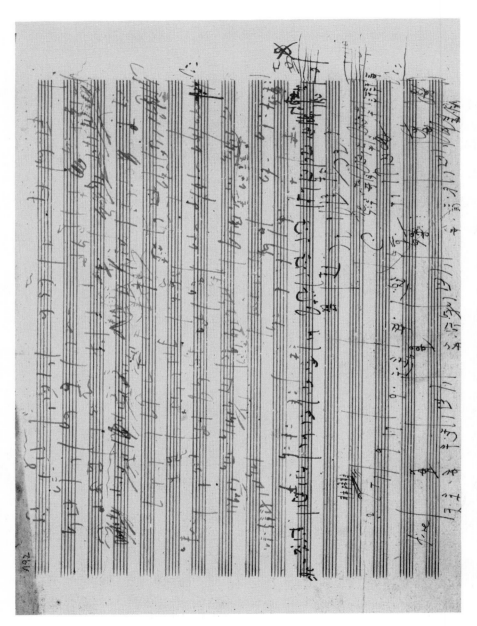

Facsimile of Mendelssohn 15, p. 192

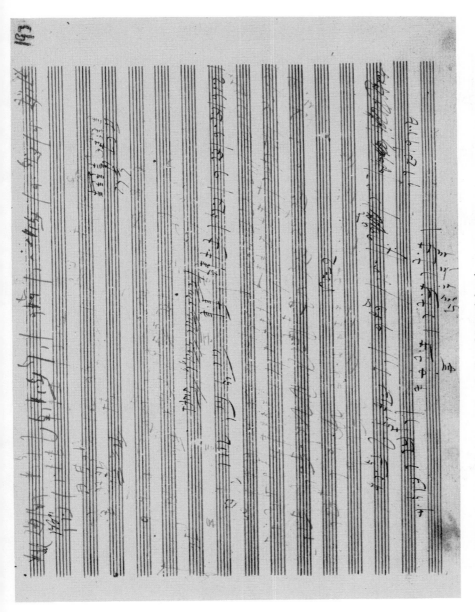

Facsimile of Mendelssohn 15, p. 193

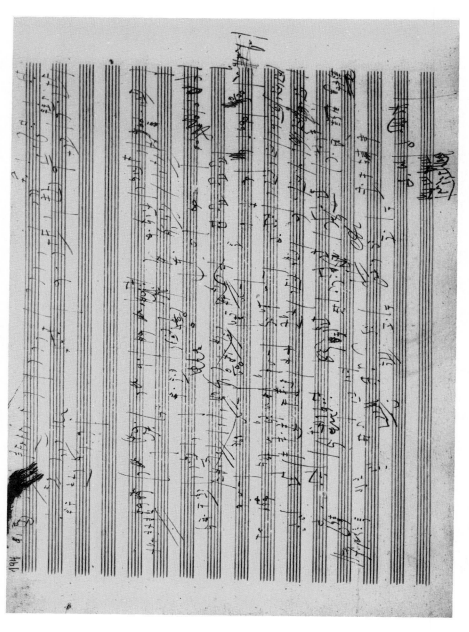

Facsimile of Mendelssohn 15, p. 194

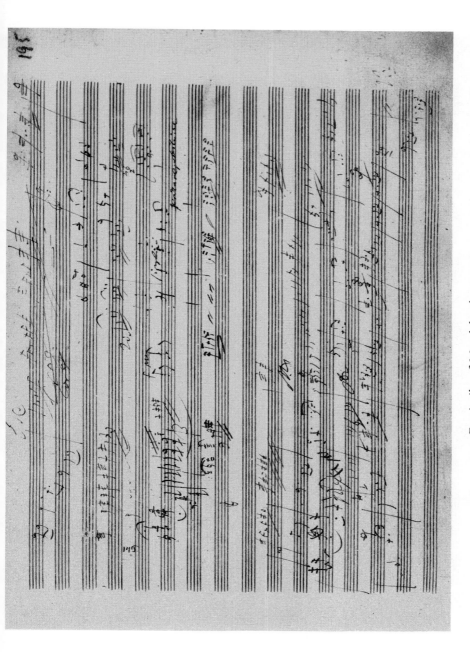

Facsimile of Mendelssohn 15, p. 195

Facsimile of Mendelssohn 15, p. 196

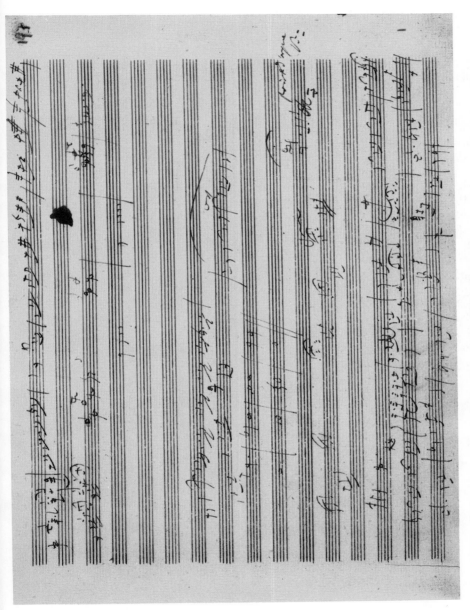

Facsimile of Mendelssohn 15, p. 197

Facsimile of Mendelssohn 15, p. 198

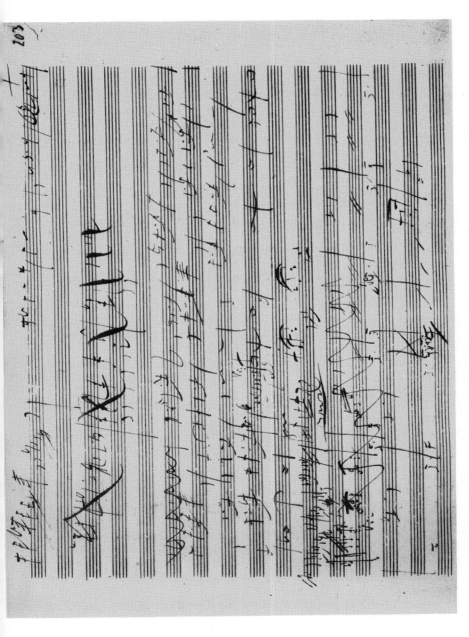

Facsimile of Mendelssohn 15, p. 203

Select Bibliography

ALBRECHT, OTTO, 'Beethoven's Autographs in the United States, in Kurt Dorfmüller (ed.), *Beiträge zur Beethoven Bibliographie: Studien und Materialien zum Werkverzeichnis von Kinsky-Halm* (Munich, 1978), 1–11.

ALBRECHT, THEODORE, 'Beethoven's *Leonore*: A New Compositional Chronology', *Journal of Musicology*, 7 (1989), 165–90.

ALDWELL, EDWARD, and SCHACHTER, CARL, *Harmony and Voice Leading* (2nd edn., New York, 1989).

ANDERSON, EMILY, (ed. and trans.), *The Letters of Beethoven*, i (New York, 1961).

BEETHOVEN, LUDWIG VAN, *Klavier-Sonaten*, ed. B. A. Wallner (Munich, 1952–3).

—— *Sonate F-Moll Opus 57 (Appassionata)*, facsimile ed. of the autograph (Leipzig: Peters, 1970).

—— *Kesslersches Skizzenbuch*, ed. Sieghard Brandenburg (Bonn, facsimile, 1976; transcription, 1978).

BLAGOY, D., 'Appassionata', *Sovetskaja muzyka*, 34 (1970), 78–92.

BRANDENBURG, SIEGHARD, 'Beethovens "Erste Entwürfe" zu Variationenzyklen', in Carl Dahlhaus *et al.* (eds.), *Bericht über den internationalen musikwissenschaftlichen Kongress Bonn 1970* (Kassel, 1971), 108–11.

—— 'The Historical Background to the "Heiliger Dankgesang" in Beethoven's A-minor Quartet Op. 132', in *Beethoven Studies*, iii, ed. Alan Tyson (Cambridge, 1982), 161–91.

CARPENTER, PATRICIA, '*Grundgestalt* as Tonal Function', *Music Theory Spectrum*, 3 (1983), 15–38.

CHURGIN, BATHIA, Review of *Ludwig van Beethoven: Kesslersches Skizzenbuch*, ed. Sieghard Brandenburg (q.v.), *Israel Studies in Musicology*, 3 (1983), 171–7.

—— 'Beethoven's Sketches for his String Quintet Op. 29', in Edward H. Roesner and Eugene K. Wolf (eds.) *Studies in Musical Sources and Style: Essays in Honor of Jan LaRue*, (Madison, Wisconsin, 1990), 441–79).

—— and BRAUN, JOACHIM, *A Report Concerning the Authentic Performance of Beethoven's Fourth Symphony, Op. 60* (Research Project of the Beethoven Seminar at Bar-Ilan University, 1976–7; Ramat Gan, 1977).

COLE, MALCOLM, 'Techniques of Surprise in the Sonata-Rondo of Beethoven', *Studia musicologica*, 12 (1970), 233–62.

—— 'Rondo', in *The New Grove Dictionary of Music and Musicians*, ed. Stanley Sadie (London, 1980), xvi. 172–7.

COOPER, BARRY 'The Evolution of the First Movement of Beethoven's "Waldstein" Sonata', *Music and Letters*, 58 (1977), 170–91.

—— 'The Origins of Beethoven's D Minor Sonata Op. 31 No. 2', *Music and Letters*, 62 (1981), 261–80.

CZERNY, CARL, *On the Proper Performance of All Beethoven's Works for the Piano*; chs. 2 and 3 of *The Complete Theoretical and Practical Piano Forte School*, Op. 500, iv; facsimile of the English edn. (London, 1842), ed. Paul Badura-Skoda (Vienna, 1970).

DRABKIN, WILLIAM, 'A Study of Beethoven's Opus 111 and its Sources', Ph.D. dissertation (Princeton University, 1977).

EINSTEIN, ALFRED, 'Neuausgaben alter Musikwerke', *Zeitschrift für Musikwissenschaft*, 10 (1927–8), 61–2.

EPSTEIN, DAVID, *Beyond Orpheus: Studies in Musical Structure* (Cambridge, Mass., 1979).

FROHLICH, MARTHA, 'Beethoven's Piano Sonatas Op. 54 and Op. 57: A Study of the Manuscript Sources', Ph.D. dissertation (Bah Ilan University, 1987).

GOSSETT, PHILIP, 'Beethoven's Sixth Symphony: Sketches for the First Movement', *Journal of the American Musicological Society*, 27 (1974), 248–84.

GREENFIELD, DONALD, 'Sketch Studies for Three Movements of Beethoven's String Quartets, Op. 18 Nos. 1 and 2', Ph.D. dissertation (Princeton University, 1983).

JOHNSON, DOUGLAS, '1794–1795: Decisive Years in Beethoven's Early Development', in *Beethoven Studies*, iii, ed. Alan Tyson (Cambridge, 1982), 1–28.

—— and TYSON, ALAN, 'Reconstructing Beethoven's Sketchbooks', *Journal of the American Musicological Society*, 25 (1972), 137–56.

—— —— and WINTER, ROBERT, *The Beethoven Sketchbooks: History, Reconstruction, Inventory* (Berkeley and Oxford, 1985).

KERMAN, JOSEPH (ed.), *Ludwig van Beethoven: Autograph Miscellany from circa 1786 to 1799* (the 'Kafka Sketchbook') (London, 1970).

—— 'Notes on Beethoven's Codas', in *Beethoven Studies iii*, ed. Alan Tyson (Cambridge, 1982), 141–59.

—— and TYSON, ALAN, *The New Grove Beethoven* (New York, 1983).

KINDERMAN, WILLIAM, 'The Evolution and Structure of Beethoven's "Diabelli" Variations', *Journal of the American Musicological Society*, 35 (1982), 306–28.

KINSKY, GEORG, *Das Werk Beethovens: Thematisch-bibliographisches Verzeichnis seiner sämtlichen vollendeten Kompositionen*, completed and ed. Hans Halm (Munich and Duisburg, 1955).

KIRKENDALE, WARREN, *Fugue and Fugato in Rococo and Classic Chamber Music*, trans. Margaret Bent and the author (2nd edn., Durham, 1979).

KLEIN, HANS-GÜNTER, *Ludwig van Beethoven: Autographe und Abschriften* (Staatsbibliothek Preussischer Kulturbesitz: Kataloge der Musikabteilung i/2; Berlin, 1975).

KRAMER, RICHARD, 'The Sketches for Beethoven's Op. 30 Violin Sonatas: History, Transcription, Analysis', Ph.D. dissertation (Princeton University, 1973).

—— 'Notes to Beethoven's Education', *Journal of the American Musicological Society*, 28 (1975), 72–101.

—— 'On the Dating of Two Aspects in Beethoven's Notation for Piano', in

Rudolf Klein (ed.), *Beethoven-Kolloquium Vienna 1977* (Kassel, 1978), 160–73.

—— ' "Das Organische der Fuge": On the Autograph of Beethoven's String Quartet in F Major, Op. 59 No. 1', in Christoph Wolff (ed.), *The String Quartets of Haydn, Mozart and Beethoven* (Cambridge, Mass., 1980), 223–65.

LaRue, Jan, *Guidelines for Style Analysis* (New York, 1970).

—— 'Sinfonia, 2', in *The New Grove Dictionary of Music and Musicians*, ed. Stanley Sadie (London, 1980), xvii. 337.

Leicher-Olbrich, Anneliese, *Untersuchungen zu Originalausgaben Beethovenscher Klavierwerke* (Wiesbaden, 1976).

Levy, Janet, *Beethoven's Compositional Choices: The Two Versions of Op. 18 No. 1, First Movement* (Philadelphia, 1982).

Lockwood, Lewis, 'On Beethoven's Sketches and Autographs: Some Problems of Definition and Interpretation', *Acta musicologica*, 42 (1970), 32–47.

—— 'The Autograph of the First Movement of Beethoven's Sonata for Violoncello and Pianoforte, Op. 69', in *The Music Forum*, ii, eds. William Mitchell and Felix Salzer (New York, 1970), 1–109.

—— 'Beethoven's Earliest Sketches for the Eroica Symphony', *Musical Quarterly*, 67 (1981), 457–78.

—— 'Beethoven's Early Works for Violoncello and Pianoforte: Innovation in Context', *Beethoven Newsletter*, 1 (1986), 17–21.

—— 'Beethoven and the Problem of Closure: Some Examples from the Middle-Period Chamber Music', in Sieghard Brandenburg and Helmut Loos (eds.), *Beethoven-Symposion, Bonn 1984* (Munich, 1987), 254–72.

Lubin, Steven, 'Techniques for the Analysis of Development in Middle-Period Beethoven', Ph.D. dissertation (New York University, 1974).

Matthews, Denis, *Beethoven's Sketchbooks: The Piano Sonatas* (Discourse Records; Tunbridge Wells, 1974), disc 7.

Meredith, William, 'The Sources for Beethoven's Piano Sonata in E Major, Op. 109', Ph.D. dissertation (University of North Carolina at Chapel Hill, 1985).

Mies, Paul, *Beethoven's Sketches: An Analysis of his Style Based on a Study of his Sketchbooks*, trans. Doris L. Mackinnon (London, 1929; repr. New York, 1974).

Newman, William S., 'Beethoven's Piano versus his Piano Ideals', *Journal of the American Musicological Society*, 23 (1970), 484–504.

—— 'The Performance of Beethoven's Trills', *Journal of the American Musicological Society*, 29 (1976), 439–62.

Nottebohm, Gustav, *Ein Skizzenbuch von Beethoven* (Leipzig, 1865); trans. Jonathan Katz in *Two Beethoven Sketchbooks* (London, 1979), 9–43.

—— 'Ein Skizzenbuch aus dem Jahre 1804', in *Zweite Beethoveniana* (Leipzig, 1887; repr. New York, 1970), 409–59.

Obelkevich, Mary Rowen, 'The Growth of a Musical Idea—Beethoven's Opus 96', *Current Musicology*, 11 (1971), 91–114.

RATNER, LEONARD, *Classic Music: Expression, Form, and Style* (New York, 1980).

RÉTI, RUDOLF, *Thematic Patterns in the Sonatas of Beethoven*, ed. Deryck Cooke (New York, 1967).

REYNOLDS, CHRISTOPHER, 'Beethoven's Sketches for the Variations in E♭, Op. 35', in *Beethoven Studies*, iii, ed. Alan Tyson (Cambridge, 1982), 47–84.

—— 'Ends and Means in the Second Finale to Beethoven's Op. 30 No. 1', in Lewis Lockwood and Phyllis Benjamin (eds.), *Beethoven Essays: Studies in Honor of Elliot Forbes* (Cambridge, Mass., 1984), 127–45.

RIEZLER, WALTER, *Beethoven* (Berlin and Zurich, 1936; Eng. trans. 1938; repr. New York, 1972).

RIVERA, BENITO V. 'Rhythmic Organization in Beethoven's Seventh Symphony', *19th-Century Music*, 6 (1983), 241–51.

ROSEN, CHARLES, *The Classical Style* (New York, 1971).

ROSENBLUM, SANDRA P., *Performance Practices in Classic Piano Music* (Bloomington, 1988).

SCHACHTER, CARL, 'Beethoven's Sketches for the First Movement of Op. 14, No. 1: A Study in Design', *Journal of Music Theory*, 26 (1982), 1–21.

SCHENKER, HEINRICH, 'Beethoven: Sonata Opus 57', *Tonwille*, 7 (1924), 3–33.

SCHMID, EDMUND, 'Beethovens *Appassionata*: Ein Vergleich zwischen Autograph und Drucktexten', *Schweizerische Musikzeitung*, 79 (1939), 161–6.

SCHMIDT-GÖRG, JOSEPH, 'Die Wasserzeichen in Beethovens Notenpapieren', in Kurt Dorfmüller (ed.), *Beiträge zur Beethoven Bibliographie: Studien und Materialien zum Werkverzeichnis von Kinsky-Halm* (Munich, 1978), 167–95.

SCHWARTZ, JUDITH, 'Opening Themes in Opera Overtures of Johann Adolf Hasse: Some Aspects of Thematic Structural Evolution in the Eighteenth Century', in Edward Clinkscale and Claire Brook (eds.) *A Musical Offering: Essays in Honor of Martin Bernstein* (New York, 1977), 243–59.

SHEER, MIRIAM, 'The Role of Dynamics in Beethoven's Instrumental Works', Ph.D. dissertation (Bar-Ilan University, 1989).

SHAMGAR, BETH, 'Dramatic Devices in the Retransition of Beethoven's Piano Sonatas', *Israel Studies in Musicology*, 2 (1980), 63–75.

SOLOMON, MAYNARD, *Beethoven* (New York, 1977).

Thayer's Life of Beethoven, rev. and ed. Elliot Forbes (Princeton, 1964; repr. 1970).

THOMPSON, HAROLD, 'An Évolutionary View of Neapolitan Formations in Beethoven's Pianoforte Sonatas', *College Music Symposium*, 20 (1980), 144–62.

TOVEY, DONALD FRANCIS, *A Companion to Beethoven's Pianoforte Sonatas*, (London, 1935).

TYSON, ALAN, 'Moscheles and his "Complete Edition" of Beethoven', *Music Review*, 25 (1964), 136–41.

—— 'Beethoven's Heroic Phase', *Musical Times*, 110 (1969), 139–41.

—— 'Notes on Five of Beethoven's Copyists', *Journal of the American Musicological Society*, 23 (1970), 439–71.

—— 'The 1803 Version of Beethoven's *Christus am Oelberge*', *Musical Quarterly*, 56 (1970), 551–84.

—— 'Stages in the Composition of Beethoven's Piano Trio Op. 70 No. 1', *Proceedings of the Royal Musical Association*, 97 (1970–1), 1–19.

—— 'Steps to Publication and Beyond', in Denis Arnold and Nigel Fortune (eds.), *The Beethoven Companion* (London, 1971), 459–89.

—— 'The Problem of Beethoven's "First" Leonore Overture', *Journal of the American Musicological Society*, 28 (1975), 292–334.

—— 'Das Leonoreskizzenbuch (Mendelssohn 15): Probleme der Rekonstruktion und der Chronologie', *Beethoven Jahrbuch*, ix (1977), 469–99.

—— 'In questa tomba oscura', in Harry Goldschmidt (ed.), *Bericht über den Internationalen Beethoven-Kongress Berlin 1977* (Leipzig, 1978), 239–45.

—— 'The "Razumovsky" Quartets: Some Aspects of the Sources', in *Beethoven Studies*, iii, ed. Alan Tyson (Cambridge, 1982), 107–40.

—— 'Ferdinand Ries (1784–1838): The History of his Contribution to Beethoven Bibliography', *19th-Century Music*, 7 (1984), 209–22.

UHDE, JÜRGEN, *Beethovens Klaviermusik*, iii (Stuttgart, 1974).

UNGER, MAX, *Beethovens Handschrift* (Bonn, 1926).

WADE, RACHEL W., 'Beethoven's Eroica Sketchbook', *Fontes artis musicae*, 24 (1977), 254–89.

WEBSTER, JAMES, 'Traditional Elements in Beethoven's Middle-Period String Quartets', in Robert Winter and Bruce Carr (eds.), *Beethoven, Performers, and Critics: The International Beethoven Congress Detroit, 1977* (Detroit, 1980), 94–133.

WEGELER, FRANZ, and RIES, FERDINAND, *Biographische Notizen über Ludwig van Beethoven* (Coblenz, 1838; facsimile of the original edition, Hildesheim, 1972).

Index of Names and Works